D0309641

# Fighting Talk

# Fighting Talk

*Flimsy Facts, Sweeping Statements and Inspired Sporting Hunches*

with Johnny Vaughan
and Colin Murray

HODDER

First published in Great Britain in 2008 by Hodder & Stoughton
An Hachette Livre UK company

3

Copyright © World's End Television Ltd. 2008

A CIP catalogue record for this title is available from the British Library

ISBN 978 0340 97755 2

Typeset in MetaPlus by Ellipsis Books Limited, Glasgow

Edited by Will Buckley

Printed and bound by Clays Ltd, St Ives plc

Hodder & Stoughton policy is to use papers that are natural, renewable and
recyclable products and made from wood grown in sustainable forests. The
logging and manufacturing processes are expected to conform to the
environmental regulations of the country of origin.

Hodder & Stoughton Ltd
338 Euston Road
London NW1 3BH

www.hodder.co.uk

This book is dedicated to the Armchair Warrior

# A

**AARON, HANK:** When chasing Babe Ruth's home run record he received plenty of encouraging mail from the great American public. Example: 'Dear Nigger Henry, You are (not) going to break this record established by the great Babe Ruth if I can help it . . . Whites are far more superior than jungle bunnies . . . My gun is watching your every black move.'

**ABBOTT, RUSS:** Gazza once told the President of Roma he was a dead ringer for Russ Abbott. Surprisingly Il Presidente was a fan of the gangly comedian and the pair bonded by playing out some of his better routines.

**ABRAMOVICH, ROMAN:** Sweet-hearted Russian geezer with a deep fondness for the game. Think Lev Yashin with both legs. At his happiest in the back seat allowing other people to express themselves. Very free with his yacht. Made something of a horlicks of his divorce from the first Mrs Abramovich as his ex ended up with a mansion on every continent, a significant percentage of Russia's natural resources and a billion or two a year spending money, while Roman was lumbered with Andriy Schevchenko, his wage bill, and the childcare. That said, he is considered by many to have single-handedly ruined English football. And could have you killed like that. Favourite gnomic saying: 'What's the difference between a rat and a pet mouse? Public relations.'

**ADAMS, TONY:** Once said to Nick Hornby 'I don't drink, I don't smoke, I don't do anything, so I'm going to have a custard cream when I want and bugger you.' Hornby made his excuses and left. Has also said: 'Sometimes the hardest thing in the world is admitting you need help. Unlike an opposing centre forward, I finally realised my addiction wasn't something I could tackle on my own' (see Marco van Basten, 1988 European Championships, England 0 Holland 3). Not only a great centre-back, but a great role model. On and off the pitch knows how to ask the question.

Arsenal – Apps: 504 Goals: 32
England – Apps: 66 Goals: 5
PFA Young Player of the Year 1987
Days (calculated one at a time) since last drink: 4,836

**ADAMS, VICTORIA:** While watching Sky Sports Super Sunday on satellite in the Bangkok Hilton turned to fellow band member, Scary, and said, 'You see that bloke who can't beat a man and has no left foot – I'm going to marry him.'

£140,500; The amount handed to George Graham in £50 notes by football agent Rune Hauge. George's response: 'I thought Jesus . . . It's a fantastic Christmas present.'

**ADEN, THE BRITISH GOVERNOR IN:** When enjoying a quiet drink with Denis Healey said, as the British prepared to leave, 'The Empire will be remembered for only two things – the game of soccer and the expression "fuck off".'

**A FORCE:** 'From now on I would like to be known as "A force".' Audley Harrison.

**AFTERSHAVE:** Bolton's J Lloyd Samuel says, 'I love aftershave! I've got a huge collection, between 30 and 40. If anyone goes away I tell them to bring some back for me. Sander For Men is my favourite.'

**AIR MILES:** 'I've probably flown more air miles than any human being; I'm starting out on my fifteenth million mile. If you take a business executive who represents a company of substance it would be considered to be abnormal if he flew for 25 or 30 years. I've been flying for 54 years.' Gary Player.

**AMERICAN PRESIDENTS:** 'I've had the good fortune to meet all of the Presidents back to Eisenhower,' says Ray Floyd. 'I met President Eisenhower and President Carter, who was not a golfer. And I've played golf with President Ford, President Clinton, President Bush, Governor Bush and Ronald Reagan. If I had to partner one in a Ryder Cup fourball it would have to be the young President Bush. Although Ford and the elder Bush were both highly competitive.'

Six foot one and a quarter inches: 'The perfect height for a darter,' says Sid Waddell.

**ANDREWS, JANE:** (born Cleethorpes) friend of Fergie (Duchess of York). She killed her lover by repeatedly hitting him over the head with a cricket bat (make unspecified) and then repeatedly stabbing him. Her defence was that her boyfriend had been responsible for his own death as he had stupidly contrived to sever an artery while removing the knife from his chest. She was found guilty.

**ANTUNES, JOSE 'FUMCA':** His career at Colchester lasted ten minutes before he was knocked unconscious on his debut by a Manchester City defender, carted off to hospital and never seen in

Essex again. He had been dubbed 'the world's best non-capped Brazilian'. He remains uncapped.

**ARDILES, OSSIE:** Small footballer immortalised in rhyme by Chas & Dave. Despite lack of size, rose above the Falklands War with aplomb.

> **Scored 2nd goal in thrilling 4–4 draw in 1981 POW escape drama** *Escape to Victory*.
> **Teams Managed:** 14
> **Favoured Number of Forwards:** 5 (although once when chasing a game at Swindon employed a 2-1-7 formation)

**ARGENTINA:** 'I believe that if we hadn't lost to Argentina, we could have gone on to win the World Cup in 1998,' claimed Paul Ince. (Hard to fault his logic, they were obviously unfortunate to be beaten by the team who were beaten by the team who were beaten by the team who were beaten by the team who won the World Cup. That being two more 'who's' than there were converted penalties against Argentina.)

**AUTOMATIC CAR WASH:** Inspirational manager Tommy 'The Doc' Docherty was very fortunate to avoid serious injury having carelessly become embroiled with an ACW.

**AYER, AJ:** Mike Tyson, Naomi Campbell and Professor AJ Ayer were at a party. Tyson, by Ayer's high standards, started pestering Campbell so he approached him to point this out. The pugilist was not amused. 'Do you know who the fuck I am?' he asked rhetorically before continuing, 'I'm the Heavyweight Champion of the World.' 'And I am the former Wykeham Professor of Logic,' replied Ayer. 'We are both pre-eminent in our field. I suggest that we step outside and talk about this like rational men.'

# Q&A

**NAME:** Johnny Vaughan

Fighting Talk *founding father and first presenter of the show, Johnny shot to fame on* Moviewatch *and as the nation's favourite breakfast TV presenter with* The Big Breakfast. *He is an all-round sports nut but Chelsea football club remains closest to his heart and he is a regular down at Stamford Bridge. He currently presents the breakfast show on Capital Radio in London.*

**PROUDEST *FIGHTING TALK* MOMENT?:** *Fighting Talk* is the only format show I've developed and gone on to host and at the time everything I did at the BBC was under considerable Press scrutiny, so I felt under a lot of pressure. The fact that both the style and tone were a radical departure for the station and it occupied a slot made sacred to fans by the likes of Baker and Kelly and Wright and Bright only added more pounds per square inch to this pressure. For the first few weeks opinion was divided – there is always hostility towards the new and different – but then along came Jim White's review in the *Daily Telegraph* and frankly I couldn't have hoped for a better piece. Here was one of broadcast sport's leading opinion formers giving us the strongest endorsement I've ever read. That was a very proud moment – and came as a massive relief.

**WHAT ARE THE SKILLS NEEDED FOR *FIGHTING TALK*?:** Wit, intelligence, brevity and originality.

**FAVOURITE *FIGHTING TALK* PANELLIST?:** Keith Allen can argue the case for pretty well anything with an outrage, sincerity or hilarity completely at odds with the tone of the question. Second favourite would have to be Dickie Davies, who always guarantees a great atmosphere in the studio.

**FAVOURITE SOUND EFFECT?:** And on, and on, and on, and on . . .

**FAVOURITE *FIGHTING TALK* QUESTION?:** It's got to be 'Who is the best-looking footballer of all time?' from the first Christmas special because it provoked my favourite ever heated argument. The panel was Jimmy Hill, Keith Allen, Dickie Davies and The Doc, and they all treated it like a very serious sporting question indeed. To hear them argue the case for their choices really was a treat. Everything *Fighting Talk* is about.

**FAVOURITE *FIGHTING TALK* ANSWER?:** Graham Taylor arguing the case for himself as England manager while defending the indefensible.

**MOMENT WHEN YOU THOUGHT *FT* WAS MOST LIKELY TO BE TAKEN OFF AIR?:** Stuart Hall's take on the problems in the Middle East.

**BIGGEST LIE TOLD ON *FIGHTING TALK*?:** A lot of Sean Lock's arguments backed up by the line, 'A lot of people don't know this right? But . . .' have turned out to be fiction – often instantly.

**AFTER FOOTBALL WHAT SPORT DO YOU THINK MAKES FOR THE BEST BITS OF *FIGHTING TALK*?:** Boxing. It's Bunce's specialist field and I love to see him showboat his expertise with typically frenzied evangelical zeal. When he's finished he always likes to look round to see the impact of his demagoguery on the faces of the panel. Sadly he mistakes wide-eyed wonderment at his bulging veins and purple face for awestruck enlightenment.

**WHICH WORD OR PHRASE IS MOST OVERUSED ON *FIGHTING TALK*?:** Influx.

**WHAT IS YOUR GREATEST *FIGHTING TALK* REGRET?:** With more Fighting Talk, I could have done more *Fighting Talk*.

**WHAT WOULD BE YOUR *FIGHTING TALK* INTRO MUSIC?:** 'Kashmir' – Led Zep or Sportsnight (sport's greatest ever theme).

**FANTASY 'DEFEND THE INDEFENSIBLE' (WHO IT WOULD BE AND WHAT WOULD THEY HAVE TO DEFEND?):** Peter Shilton. 'Despite my superior height, much longer arms, and the advantage of being able to legitimately use my hands, back in Mexico 86 there was no way I could have out-jumped Maradona to punch the ball away. I never stood a chance.'

**ANY OTHER BUSINESS:** I know the old First Division Cup belongs to the Football League and the FA runs the Premiership, but regardless of who does the admin, or what they are called, the top division champions should get their names on the same trophy as the great sides that went before them. I don't see why the champions of the top division of the oldest Football League in the world should have to lift a trophy lacking either the proud tradition, sentimental weight or the historical significance of the original cup, which is now awarded to the second division champs. Aside from the fact the Premiership Trophy looks like it came from a shoe repairer's/key cutting shop, how can a trophy that should be one of the most sacred objects in the footballing world be downgraded? The whole point of being champions is that you get your club's name engraved on a trophy along with the legendary teams of the past. The current one dates back to 1992 and has four clubs on it. Do you think the R&A would change the Claret Jug?

**WHICH FOOTBALL TEAM DO YOU SUPPORT?:** The Chelsea
Football Club.

**WHICH SPORTING PERSON DO YOU MOST IDENTIFY WITH?:**
Matt Le Tissier.

**FAVOURITE PERSON IN SPORT?:** Zola.

**LEAST FAVOURITE PERSON IN SPORT?:** Frank Rijkard because of
the spitting thing. I just can't forget it.

**PROUDEST PERSONAL SPORTING MOMENT?:** Hole in one at
Stoke Park on Bobby Moore Charity Day. It was organised by
Spoony and it was the nearest to the pin hole so I was able to put
my marker in the hole. His was only a foot away.

**MOST EMBARRASSING SPORTING MOMENT?:** Falling over
during the 100m hurdles when I was 12 at school sports day. I
tripped between hurdles.

**WHAT IS YOUR MOST TREASURED SPORTING POSSESSION?:**
Zola's shirt from a European Cup away game. Mark Bright got it for
me and it had an authentic hum of matchday BO.

**GIVE ME YOUR BEST SPORTING STATISTIC:** The Chelsea/Leeds
FA Cup final replay in 1970 was seen by more people on TV than
any other sporting event in British TV history. 30 million.

**STRANGEST INJURY SUFFERED ON A SPORTS FIELD?:** Dislocated
knee while jumping up to try and touch the crossbar of the school
rugby posts.

**WORST SPORTING BET YOU HAVE MADE TO DATE?:** Only
putting five pounds on a horse I'd been given a tip on that romped
home by 8 lengths at 12–1.

**WHAT IS YOUR FAVOURITE SPORTING OCCUPATION?:** These days golf, but I love taking my son to football training.

**WHAT DO YOU DISLIKE IN A SPORTSPERSON?:** Going down at the slightest touch instead of going for goal.

**WHAT IS YOUR FAVOURITE SPORTING MOTTO?:** Cheer us on through the sun and rain.

# The *Fighting Talk* Award for Tilting at Windmills

**MAURICE FLITCROFT:** Chain-smoking shipyard operative. In 1976, aged 46, he bought a half-set of clubs and set out to find 'fame and fortune' by playing in the Open at Royal Birkdale against 'Jack Nicklaus and all that.' Wisely, to help him in his ambition he borrowed a Peter Allis instruction manual from the local library and read a couple of articles by Al Geiberger. Declaring himself a professional on the entry form, he was invited to play at the Formby qualifier. He shot a disappointing 49 over par (the worst score in Open history).

His playing partner, Jim Howard, recalls, 'After gripping the club like he was intent on murdering someone, Flitcroft hoisted it straight up, it came down vertically, and the ball travelled precisely four feet. We put that one down to nerves, but after he shanked a second one we called the R&A officials.' Under the rules of the tournament, however, nothing could be done. 'It wasn't funny at the time,' explained Howard.

Flitcroft explained to the waiting press that he had been suffering from 'lumbago and fibrositis, but I don't want to make excuses.' He also mentioned that he was 'an expert with a four wood, deadly' but, such were his nerves on making his Open debut, he had stupidly left it behind in the car.

In 1977, an application, in his own name, was turned down. Undaunted, in 1978, posing as American pro Gene Pacecki (pronounced 'pay chequey') he finagled his way into the qualifier at South Herts only to be thrown out after a few holes.

Fail, fail better. In 1983, he showed up at Pleasington having dyed his hair and applied a false moustache, calling himself Gerald Hoppy and claiming to be a Swiss pro. He shot 63 on the outward nine, 27 over, before officials realised they had 'another Maurice Flitcroft' to deal with. 'Imagine their surprise when they discovered they had the actual Maurice Flitcroft,' said Flitcroft.

In 1990, now going by the name James Beau Jolley (pronounced 'Beaujolais') he attempted to qualify from Ormskirk. He double bogeyed the first, bogeyed the second, and was on course for an unlikely par at the third, when the R&A once again intervened. He continued playing on the beach until breaking his hip in 2001.

# Homework

Mark the following examples of homework and see if you can do better . . .

Talking about a return to Milan, Chelsea's Andriy Shevchenko is quoted as saying, 'This club is like a family to me.'

Can you suggest other sporting people that might fit into a family unit?

- Stan Collymore as 'your dad's brother' whose name is never mentioned.

- Karen Brady, managing director of Birmingham City FC, as the aunt that gets you through puberty . . .

- Delia Smith as the mullered aunty at Christmas, 'WHERE ARE YOU?!'

- David Pleat as Grandad. Slightly senile and always getting names wrong.

- . Jamie Murray as the moody teenage cousin that sulks in the corner at a family wedding then tries to get off with your sister.

- Alex Ferguson is the uncle that comes round to your house at Christmas with four cans of 8% Norseman lager and drinks all your malt whisky.

DEFEND THE INDEFENSIBLE
*Each week the two leading panellists face one final challenge to determine the winner of* Fighting Talk. *They must defend an*

*unpalatable proposition to the best of their ability for a full and fluent twenty seconds:*

I preferred South African cricket under apartheid.

*or*

The best comedy on the telly this week was the Women's FA Cup final.

ODD ONE OUT
One of the following statements about David Beckham is false. Please give the full reasoning behind your selection:

a) He ran an average of 8.8 miles in every game he played for Manchester United.

b) His first car was a Ford Escort.

c) While watching Victoria give birth to Brooklyn he enjoyed a Lion bar.

d) His middle name is David.

e) He had his 'Vihctoria' tattoo written in Hindi because, he explained, 'English would be tacky.'

# Stats

England World Cup and European Championship Official Songs
relative to Tournament Performance

........................................................................................

*1986*  'We've Got the Whole World at our Feet'
England World Cup Squad
(66 in Charts) (Quarter-finals in World Cup)

........................................................................................

*1988*  'All the Way'
England Football Team with Stock, Aitken
and Waterman (64 in Charts) (1st Round in Euro
Championships)

........................................................................................

*1990*  'World in Motion'
New Order/England National Squad
(1st in Charts) (Semi-finals in World Cup)

........................................................................................

*1996*  'Three Lions'
Baddiel, Skinner and the Lightning Seeds
(1st in Charts) (Semi-finals in Euro Championships)

........................................................................................

*1998*  '(How does it feel to be) On Top of the World'
England United (Spice Girls, Lightning Seeds and
Echo and the Bunnymen) (9th in Charts)
(2nd Round in World Cup)

........................................................................................

*2000*  'Jerusalem'
Fat Les 2000 (10th in Charts)
(1st Round in Euro Championships)

2002    'We're on the Ball'
        Ant & Dec (3rd in Charts)
        (Quarter-finals in World Cup)

2004    'All Together Now'
        The Farm feat. St Francis Xavier's Boys' Choir
        (5th in Charts) (Quarter-finals of Euro Championships)

2006    'World at your Feet'
        Embrace (3rd in Charts)
        (Quarter-finals of World Cup)

Correlation coefficient = 0.405965. When the official England song goes to number 1, England perform better in the tournament, as seen in World Cup 90 and Euro 96. Top 10 finishes for the England song in 2002, 2004 and 2006 resulted in a consistent performance of a Quarter-final finish in the tournament, but World Cup 86 bucks this trend, where the song finished 66th but England reached the Quarter-finals. And a number 10 finish in 2000 for the official song still led to England being knocked out in the 1st Round.

**BALL, ALAN:** The last member of the World Cup side to hang up his boots. Most of the teams he managed were unfortunately relegated: Blackpool, Portsmouth, Colchester, Stoke City, Exeter, Manchester City . . .

Despite this, when asked for his autograph he would write: 'Alan J Ball – WIN.'

**Matches Played:** 975
**Length of Career:** 21 years
**Clubs Represented:** 8. Everton, Arsenal, Blackpool (x2) Southampton (x2), Bristol Rovers, Vancouver Whitecaps, Philadelphia Fury, Eastern Athletic.
**Miles Covered During One Glorious Summer's Afternoon at Wembley in 1966:** 211

**BALLESTEROS, SEVERIANO:** The longest name in golf, if pronounced reverentially with the full nine syllables: Sev-er-i-an-o Ball-es-ter-os. Called Steve by Americans even when he was comfortably the greatest, and most charismatic, golfer in the world.

First European to Win a Major
Youngest Player to Win the Open in the 20th Century
20 Points out of 37 in Ryder Cup including (with JM Olazabal)
Played: 15, Won: 11, Drew: 2, Lost: 2.

**BANNING YOUR OWN TV STATION:** 'The director of communications is unhappy with the tone of some interviews,' was the reason given for Chelsea FC downsizing their own propagandists. When you don't believe your own propaganda . . .

**BARASSI CUP:** Won by Staines Town in 1975, in front of a crowd of 70,000 in Rome's Olympic stadium, when they defeated Banco di Roma. Staines, therefore, have won more European trophies than Wenger's Arsenal.

**BARCELONA:** 'I said when I arrived at Brentford that my next club would be Barcelona,' Martin Allen. In the event, his next club was Milton Keynes Dons.

**BARESI, FRANCO:** Nickname, Piscinin (Milanese for little one). 'He is the best defender of all,' says Marcel Desailly. 'There has been no one at his level. He was complete: technically, tactically and physically. He never talked a lot, only when there was something important to say. And at that moment . . . it was magnificent.' When he retired they retired his number.

> AC Milan 1977–1997 – **Apps:** 532 **Goals:** 16
> Italy 1982–1994 – **Apps:** 81 **Goals:** 1 (against Russia)

**BARKER, SUE:** Filth . . . very allegedly it is claimed that Sue was responsible for taking Tim Henman's virginity. However, no footage exists and rumours that the England number one celebrated with a trademark fist pump are unlikely to be true.

> **Highest World Ranking:** 3
> **Grand Slam Semi-Finals Reached:** 4
> **Number of Years Hosted** *A Question of Sport*: 10

£300,000: The profit Leeds made on selling Eric Cantona to Manchester United. 'Eric likes to do what he likes when he likes – and then fucks off,' said Howard Wilkinson before going on to point out that at the other United, 'perhaps he'll have a better chance of first-team games.' He used the money to part-fund the £2.9 million purchase of Brian Deane.

**BEAR-BAITING:** 'The Puritan hated bear-baiting,' wrote Lord Macaulay, 'not because it gave pain to the bear, but because it gave pleasure to the spectator.' It was not until 1835 that baiting was prohibited by Parliament and its last known occurrence was in the small town of Knottingley.

**BECKHAM, DAVID:** Arguably the most happily married sportsman in world football. The Beckhams have three fridges, one of which, on David's orders, is exclusively used for salad. 'David is so from another planet,' says his wife Victoria. 'I mean what is he like?' David Beckham is Google's most searched sports topic 2003 and 2004, Celebrity Dad of the Year 2005–2007. (A run of success which saw him getting to keep the coveted 'Golden Nappy' trophy.)

**BERBICK, TREVOR:** The last man to fight Muhammad Ali. He then came up against Mike Tyson. 'Big punchers don't worry me,' he said before the fight. 'It's the artistic guys that give me something to think about.' He was knocked out in the second round. 'Everything he's got has "goodnight" written all over it,' said the referee Mills Lane about Tyson. Trevor called himself The Soldier of the Cross and once surprised promoter Don King by appearing in his room holding a Bible, wearing a large crucifix and saying, 'The Lord is on your side. Only with thine eyes shalt thou behold and see the reward of the wicked.' In 1992, he was sentenced to five years in prison for raping the family babysitter.

**BERG, PATTY:** Arguably the greatest women golfer of all time, she won 15 majors and was the first woman to play without a hat. Born in Minneapolis in 1918 she represented the otherwise all-male 50th Street Tigers as a quarterback. Switching to golf she won the US Amateur at the age of 20 and promptly turned pro. A brave decision given the almost complete lack of professional tournaments. A serious car crash kept her out of competition for 18 months. However on her return she won two tournaments in succession and promptly joined the Marines. The fifties were her golden decade as she won four World Championships in five years.

**BLAH, BLAH, BLAH:** 'Our training is strong. Is modern. Training wins also. I have 21 trophies. There is blah, blah, blah from you. Fools write who know nothing. Blah, blah, blah, blah. I can understand people paying. No problema. Let whistle. Is right. Have lost. But run 90 minutes! I am a professional in psychology. We train, make fitness. You people always make qua, qua, qua. Shit fools!' Irish manager Giovanni Trapattoni keeping the press on side while coach of Red Bull Salzburg.

**BLISSETT, LUTHER:** Remains one of football's enduring mysteries. While playing for Milan, Luther scored five goals in 30 games and, according to one Italian newspaper, was 'famous for missing open goals and for the inexorable precision with which he would find the goalpost.' His name lives on in Italy, however, for reasons of anarchy. In 1997 four men went on trial in Rome for travelling on a train without tickets. When asked to identify themselves, all said they were Luther Blissett and argued that 'a collective identity does not need a ticket'. They explained that they chose Blissett because he was 'just a nice Afro-Caribbean guy who had problems with the Italian way of playing football.'

Overall Club Record 1975–1994 – **Apps:** 584 **Goals:** 213
England, 1982–1984 – **Apps:** 14 **Goals:** 3

**BORG, BJORN:** The first man to win the Wimbledon Gentlemen's Singles and then claim, 'The world is my sauna.'

> Career Record – Wins: 587 Losses: 124
> Career Titles: 97
> Career Prize Money: US$ 3,655,751

**BORN NEAR BARKING:** Legendary sportswriter Geoffrey Mortlake really did once write: 'Though technically born near Barking I have always considered myself a proud son of Liverpool. Geography counts for less in these matters than personality and physiognomy, and if you cut me I bleed Scouse.'

166: The number of assists provided by Dennis Bergkamp during his time at Arsenal.

**BOSNICH, BREAKFAST WITH:** Before his debut – and so far only – appearance on the show, Mark Bosnich entered the BBC staff canteen and scarfed two bacon baguettes washed down with five cappuccinos and finished off with a large cigar (surely against the rules?) before appearing in the studio, laughing hysterically at anything (including the travel) and knocking back a record 12 litres of water. Now says: 'I really don't give a toss about football any more. Fuck football. I really can't be bothered. I want to try and make it as a sports star in America. I don't know what type of sports I would do. But that is what I want.'

**BOTHAM, IAN:** A knight of the realm on and off the greensward. Once drank John Arlott under the table at his home in Alderney, the great commentator not being discovered until tea the following day.

**BOTHAM, IAN (CONT.):**

Test Matches Played: 102
Runs Scored: 5200
Batting Av: 33.54
100s/50s: 14/22
Top Score: 208
Balls Bowled: 21,815
Wickets: 383
Bowling Av: 28.40

One Dayers Played: 116
Runs Scored: 2113
Batting Av: 23.21
100s/50s: 0/9
Top Score: 79
Balls Bowled: 6271
Wickets: 145
Bowling Av: 28.54
Minutes Slept during Headingley Test: 45

**BOULDY:** Asked if his Arsenal team had ever bothered marking posts at corners Tony Adams replied, 'Nah, we just used to head the ball away. Bouldy at the near, me at the far, we'd just go and head the ball away.'

**BOYCOTT, GEOFFREY:** An uncompromisingly direct ladies' man, yet he is becoming camper by the year. The pastel tank-tops he has taken to wearing being a throwback to the golden days of Lionel Blair.

Test Matches Played: 108
Runs Scored: 8114
Batting Av: 47.72
100s/50s: 22/42
Top Score: 246
Balls Bowled: 944
Wickets: 7
Bowling Av: 54.57

One Dayers Played: 36
Runs Scored: 1082
Batting Av: 36.06
100s/50s: 1/9
Top Score: 105
Balls Bowled: 168
Wickets: 5
Bowling Av: 21.00
Number of Years Modelled for Man at C&A: 7

**BRAGG, MELVYN:** 'Hassan Kachloul was here yesterday, telling us how he plans to write about Moroccan football, poverty and the Muslim faith. I'm not saying he's Melvyn Bragg, but it'll be interesting stuff.' James Freedman, Chief Executive of Icons website (where the most frequently asked question is: 'Which celebrity do you fancy most?').

**BRAZIL, BREAKFAST WITH:** The *Today* programme without the obvious left-wing bias. Sample piece of common sense: 'The Channel Tunnel should be filled with concrete to prevent further illegal immigration.' With sidekick Ronnie Irani, the former Ipswich Town front-man presides over a fast-paced, never more than entertaining show.

**BREARLEY, MIKE:** The most cerebral Test captain of the modern age. A fact never better illustrated than in the famous Headingley Test. Australia only needed 129 to win, but did 'The Professor of Philosophy' give the new ball to Bob Willis? Of course not. First, he gave it to Ian Botham and then, to Big Bob's evident chagrin, to Graham 'Picca' Dilly and then, as Bob fumed in the outfield to Chris 'Chilly' Old. Faced by such an attack Australia progressed serenely to 56 for 1. Then, and only then, did Brearley (he has a degree in people) hand the cherry to R.G.D Willis. Incandescent with rage, the Warwickshire quick responded with figures of 8 for 43. Game, Set and Test to Brears.

£5 million a goal: Corrado Grabbi's two goals for Blackburn cost £5m each. 'I love the city, the club and the fans. I am living a dream!' he said.

**BRICK WALLS:** 'There is a story I like to tell. In Japan, if you tell the players to sprint at high speed into a brick wall, they will do it unquestioningly. Then, when they crack their heads open and fall to the ground, they look at you and feel completely betrayed. The English player runs at full speed into the brick wall, gets up, dusts himself off and does it again. He won't feel betrayed by his manager or ask himself the point of running into the wall. Now, the French player, like the Italian, will react differently. He'll look at you and say, "Why don't you show us first how it's done?" You see, the thing is that they only trust the manager to a certain point. It's in the blood of the English. It's the almost military attitude with which they approach everything. They do as they're told, they follow orders, they do not question authority and they never give up. I don't think it's a coincidence that every time there is a war, the English almost always win.' Arsène Wenger.

**BROWN, JIMMY:** One morning Jimmy White woke up and decided, on a marketing whim, to change his name to Jimmy Brown. As an aide-memoire, for him and us, he started dressing in a brown suit, with a blue bow-tie, and, on occasion, a white cap so he could resemble as far as is sartorially possible a bottle of the sauce. Explaining his decision Brown said, 'The HP Sauce sponsorship of the brown ball really puts the fun back into snooker and given my previous surname I wanted to follow that lead.' Graham White (still called White at time of writing), Marketing Director of HP Sauce, added, 'Not only does it [the name-change] capture the slightly quirky British humour that so typifies snooker lovers and HP sauce users alike but it also shows an honesty and unpretentiousness by sponsoring those un-sponsorable great moments in everyday British life.' At a marketing stroke, the game once referred to as being 'not about frames, but frames of mind' had moved on to being 'not about bottle, but bottles of sauce.'

**BURGESS, SHAYNE 'BULLDOG':** Turned up for a darts tournament in Sweden with a suitcase containing 60 chicken sandwiches.

**BUSH, GEORGE:** The greatest golfer ever to hold the Presidency, having a 'legitimate' 15 handicap. It was on the first tee at the Kennebunkport golf course, that the world's most powerful man said, 'I call upon all nations to do everything they can to stop these terrorist killings. Thank you. Now, watch this drive.' He duck-hooked the drive which, with hindsight, did not augur well for the so-called War on Terror.

**BUSHTUCKER TRIALS:** The following 'big asks' were attempted by John Fashanu in his attempt to be crowned King of the Jungle.

1. The Bridge of Doom. The Fashanu verdict – 'It's hard.'

2. The Log Bog – 'I don't think that means happy days.'

3. The Eel Helmet – 'This is a silly one.'

4. Keep It In Your Pants – 'It was not nice.'

5. The Snake Pit – 'Whoever thought of that, I'd like to meet in a dark alley.'

6. Bobbing for Stars – 'Oh, god, it stinks.'

# Q&A

**NAME:** Colin Murray

*Colin has now been in the* Fighting Talk *presenter's chair longer than anyone else. He is an avid Liverpool fan and famously has five stars tattooed on his arm, one for each of Liverpool's European Cup wins. He follows the fortunes of the Toronto Blue Jays in baseball, a sport he loves. Colin presents a daily music show on BBC Radio 1 and also fronts FIVE'S domestic football coverage.*

**PROUDEST *FIGHTING TALK* MOMENT?:** Every week, to be part of such a great show. I know that's clichéd but to give up your Saturday every week, which means missing most of your teams matches, you have to be in love with it.

**WHAT ARE THE SKILLS NEEDED FOR *FIGHTING TALK*?:** Thick skin, a sense of humour and a fan's view of sport.

**FAVOURITE SOUND EFFECT?:** Different Strokes. Any time anyone talks about race in sport, my finger hovers over the button with glee. It always lightens the mood!

**FAVOURITE *FIGHTING TALK* ANSWER?:** Jim Jeffries' 'Have a go at a Yank' answer. It was just the most outrageous thing I've ever heard said, intentionally, on daytime radio. I also liked when Martin Kelner referred to his '30 years of unblemished heterosexuality'.

**BIGGEST LIE TOLD ON *FIGHTING TALK*?:** By just about every contestant . . . 'It's not about the winning.'

**AFTER FOOTBALL, WHAT SPORT DO YOU THINK MAKES FOR THE BEST BITS OF *FIGHTING TALK*?:** Football forms the backbone but it's the other sports that usually provide most humour. If I had to go for one, I would say amateur sport – when a panellist tells a personal story about their sporting past.

**IN ONE WORD – *FIGHTING TALK*?:** Family.

**WHAT IS YOUR GREATEST *FIGHTING TALK* REGRET?:** I have always wanted to do a *Fighting Talk* special, hosted by Gabby Logan, with the panellists being Johnny Vaughan, Christian O'Connell and myself.

**WHAT WOULD BE YOUR CHOICE OF *FIGHTING TALK* INTRO MUSIC?:** I would probably want Johnny Cash's version of 'Danny Boy'.

**FANTASY 'DEFEND THE INDEFENSIBLE' (WHO IT WOULD IT BE AND WHAT WOULD THEY HAVE TO DEFEND?):** John Rawling. I'd give anything to avoid my wife's cooking. We tried once with this and failed!

**ANY OTHER BUSINESS?:** At the moment, I have a bee in my bonnet about opera singers doing national anthems and the likes at big football occasions. If I want to hear Lesley Garrett sing 'Abide With Me', I'll buy a ticket to see her in the Albert Hall.

**WHICH FOOTBALL TEAM DO YOU SUPPORT?:** Liverpool and Northern Ireland.

**WHICH SPORTING PERSON DO YOU MOST IDENTIFY WITH?:** Barry McGuigan, because he knew how to be a worldwide sporting name from Northern Ireland without bringing politics or religion into it.

**FAVOURITE PERSON IN SPORT?:** Apart from Barry, it's probably David Healy and Jamie Carragher. I love them both more than any woman.

**LEAST FAVOURITE PERSON IN SPORT?:** Wow, which one? I think Roy Keane, however talented, was a thug of a footballer. And Kelly Holmes. I am sure she is a nice person, but there was a two-year period when every time I turned on my TV she was there with those two gold medals. She must have had them surgically attached to her hand.

**PROUDEST PERSONAL SPORTING MOMENT?:** Finally earning my ten-yard swimming certificate . . . when I was 28!

**MOST EMBARRASSING SPORTING MOMENT?:** I took a couple of penalties at half time of the Merseyside Derby. I was feeling great, walked down the tunnel, touched the sign, but as I entered the pitch and saw what the Kop looks like from a player's perspective, I completely shat myself. My first penalty hardly reached the goal and my second was straight out of the Stevie Wonder book of dead-ball taking.

**FIRST SPORTING MEMORY?:** Liverpool winning the European Cup against Real Madrid in 1981, although I have few memories of it these days. The 1984 final, though, I can recount the entire night.

**WHICH SPORTING SKILL WOULD YOU MOST LIKE TO HAVE?:**
I'd love to be able to hit a baseball. I'd love to hit a home run at
the Rogers Centre or anywhere else for that matter. I don't think it's
possible to be taught this skill though – I think you are born to play
baseball. Or not.

**WHAT IS YOUR MOST TREASURED SPORTING POSSESSION?:**
Probably my Istanbul Champions League Cup Final ticket, although
maybe our actual flag we had made. It's a picture of Bully from
Bullseye in a Liverpool top and the flag says 'You Can't Beat a Bit
Of Istanbully – Super, Smashing, Reds'.

**GIVE ME YOUR BEST SPORTING STATISTIC:** *Fighting Talk*'s most
successful presenter in terms of appearances . . . you know the
rest.

**STRANGEST INJURY SUFFERED ON A SPORTS FIELD?:** I once
casually stopped a guy from falling over during a five-a-side game
and the string from his shorts tangled around my finger and
snapped it in three places. I still can't straighten it to this day.

**WORSE SPORTING BET YOU HAVE MADE TO DATE?:** Where do I
start? A friend and I once thought we had come up with this great
idea – back a team to draw o–o, to draw, to have no first or last
goal scorer etc. basically, every bet would come up if the score
finished nil-nil. We placed about ten of these as accumulators and
a couple came up. We thought we'd won about fifty grand until the
betting website contacted us the next morning to inform us that we
had broken the law by making the bet.

**WHAT QUALITIES DO YOU MOST ADMIRE IN A
SPORTSPERSON?:** Honesty . . .

**WHAT SPORT SENDS YOU TO SLEEP?:** Basketball.

**WHAT'S BEEN THE BEST SPORTS EVENT YOU HAVE WITNESSED?:** I have to go for Northern Ireland beating England 1–0 at Windsor Park. The BBC asked me to do a half-time chat with them, and as I finished, David Healy walked past me, stopped, came back, and shook my hand. I was speechless. Half an hour later he scored the winning goal.

# The *Fighting Talk* Tribute for Being Too Much of a Fan

**STEVE BARTMAN:** A twenty-six-year-old global human resources company worker from Chicago, Illinois, his big mistake was to reach out to grab a souvenir ball and prevent Chicago Cubs player Moises Alou from making the final out of the innings to take the Cubs, who were leading 3–0, to the World Series for the first time since 1945. As frustrated as they were surprised by Bartman's attempted catch, the Cubs disintegrated and lost the game 8–3 to the Florida Marlins. In the build up to the now crucial deciding game of the series, Cubs' manager Dusty Baker said, 'We've got to win for that kid. For us, it's just a ball game. For him, it's the rest of his life.' His brother Martin said, 'He's really hurting right now. I love him so much I'd give up a piece of my anatomy for him.'

Bartman was swift to apologise: 'There are few words to describe how awful I feel and what I have experienced within these last 24 hours . . . I am so truly sorry from the bottom of this Cubs fan's broken heart. I ask that Cubs fans everywhere redirect the negative energy that has been vented towards my family, my friends, and myself into the usual positive support for our beloved team on their way to being National League champs.'

They lost 9–6.

Some Cubs fans were less than happy. Bartman received death threats, news cameras parked outside his front door, and his employers told him not to bother coming in. There is always an upside: in Florida Jim Robinson, the owner of The Trap, said 'We'll give him free draught beer and all the lap dances he can handle.' And Governor Jed Bush offered him asylum. 'Stuff happens,' said the President's brother.

Some Cubs fans over-reacted. Eric Neel wrote, 'We're just like Icarus today, baby, nothing but a close-but-no-cigar mess of wax and bones. The Cubs didn't lose, the Cubs are losing itself. We define the concept so that winning has meaning. We are the yard-stick, the baseline. You get me?'

# Homework

Mark the following examples of homework and see if you can do better . . .

Wayne Rooney has given up trying to learn the guitar . . . so panel, can we have your sportspeople as musical instruments please . . .

- Ronaldo. The bagpipes. Whiney. Virtually unplayable to the mere mortal. And controlled by a Scot who everyone suspects wears no pants.

- Avram Grant is a Casio keyboard. Doesn't know how to play it, just hits demo and lets it do its thing.

- Sharron Davies as a drum – you could bang her all day.

DEFEND THE INDEFENSIBLE
The best bit of the snooker is watching all the young men in tight trousers bending over the table.

*or*

Ricky Hatton is just soooo gay (to Canadian Greg Brady, long-serving panellist and father of two).

ESSAY
In a recent list published in *The Sunday Times* property section it was revealed that the Queen owned the largest number of properties in the country followed by the Duke of Westminster, the Archbishop of Canterbury and, closing fast, Robbie Fowler.

What does Fowler's meteoric rise up this list (he was not even in the top 500 a decade ago) say about social mobility in modern Britain? Discuss, with graphs.

# Stats

Real per capita GDP growth, Annual Percentage Rate, 2 years pre- and post-World Cup. *Source: Penn World Tables.*

....................................................................................................

| *1954* | Germany (champion) | 7.1 and 9.1 |
| | Switzerland (host) | 4.0 and 5.5 |
| *1958* | Brazil (champion) | 5.7 and 3.3 |
| | Sweden (host) | 1.9 and 4.0 |
| *1962* | Brazil (champion) | 3.9 and –0.8 |
| | Chile (host) | 3.2 and 1.8 |
| *1966* | England (champion and host) | 1.4 and 3.0 |
| *1970* | Brazil (champion) | 6.5 and 9.7 |
| | Mexico (host) | 2.9 and 5.2 |
| *1974* | Germany (champion and host) | 9.5 and 4.7 |
| *1978* | Argentina (champion and host) | 0.0 and 5.6 |
| *1982* | Italy (champion) | 0.3 and 1.5 |
| | Spain (host) | 0.6 and 0.5 |
| *1986* | Argentina (champion) | 0.9 and –2.4 |
| | Mexico (host) | 2.2 and 0.6 |

| *1990* | Germany (champion) | 3.3 and 1.3 |
| | Italy (host) | 2.4 and 0.9 |

*Mean*
3.6 and 3.5
2.2 and 3.2

*Median*
3.6 and 3.1
2.1 and 3.5

All of which suggest that winning the World Cup does sod all for your economy. Oddly, very few commodity brokers watch Brazil winning the World Cup on a Sunday night and then go and buy shedloads of coffee on Monday morning.

However, hosting the World Cup can give you a fillip as people of many nations flock to your country to buy a range of replica shirts.

We can therefore conclude that you are better off spending your money attempting to nobble FIFA than employing Fabio Capello and his entourage.

# C

**CALLAGHAN, NEIL:** The former Watford player always used to eat 'lucky crab' on a Friday night, hoped to 'own a small shop' as a career after playing and most wanted to meet Suzanne Dando.

**CAMPBELL, ALISTAIR:** When asked, during the run-up to an election, 'If the Labour campaign was a person, who would you want it to be?' Alistair Campbell really did reply 'Jeff Stelling' before going on to explain, 'He [Stelling, not Campbell] embodied a number of qualities essential to a campaign – stability, consistency, deep knowledge about your subject and your audience, calmness under pressure, looking and sounding authoritative, the ability to laugh when things go wrong, enthusiasm, leadership and teamwork, attention to detail, sureness of touch, as well as flair and adaptability. Very few political campaigns manage to combine all those qualities. Jeff Stelling does it every week.'

**CANTONA, ERIC DANIEL PIERRE:** The captain of the French Beach Soccer team, he scored 17 of the 19 penalties that he took for Manchester United. Scored 80 League and Cup goals for Manchester United: 56 with his right foot, 10 with his left, and 14 with his head. He played in 14 FA Cup games for Manchester United and never finished on the losing side. Won three consecutive soccer league titles for three different clubs: Marseille, Leeds United and Manchester United.

Recently appointed as Minister for Culture and Sport by President Sarkozy, he is working on a masterplan with Michel Platini to transform European football along socialist lines.

**CARLING, WILL:** Captain of England from 1988 to 1996, winning 72 caps, he was the youngest ever England captain at the age of 22 and, coincidentally, also the youngest man to befriend Princess Diana. A school contemporary remembers a 'steady string of pretty similar-looking girlfriends. The pattern of the blonde model was established very early on.'

He asked for his psychology dissertation – all eight double-spaced pages of it – to be removed from Durham University library because students were reading it, not for educational enlightenment, but for pure entertainment.

**CARNEGIE HALL:** 'A great violinist doesn't want to stay in Podunk, Kansas, he wants to play Carnegie Hall. I want to prove how good I am.' Black pitcher Paige Satchel talking to Lester 'Red' Rodney in 1937 and confirming that he no longer wanted to be 'a frog in a small puddle' and did want to play in the Major Leagues.

**CASTROL:** 'It is exciting to be working with Castrol,' says David Beckham. 'I'm thrilled to be endorsing a brand that signifies top performance and leadership; qualities that are important in playing football – and in life.'

**CAUTHEN, STEVE:** In 1977, aged 17, 'Stevie Wonder' was the first jockey to be named *Sports Illustrated* Sportsman of the Year. 'I was an overnight success who had been working at being an overnight success for many years,' says Cauthen. 'That boy could ride a swamp-hog naked through the Louisiana bayous and still win by twenty-five lengths,' says JT Lundy, President of Calumet Farm.

**CELEBRITY:** The celebrity that Coventry's Don Hutchinson most fancies 'changes daily but today it would be . . . Cameron Diaz.' He would like Sean Bean to play him in a story of his life.

**CENTURY:** 'Any club can have a bad century.' Chicago Cubs manager.

**CHANCE:** 'The fact that Bruno is going into the ring with me is taken by some people to mean that he has a chance. In fact, it really means he has no chance. I'm not normally a hostile person but I have to say he's in trouble, real trouble.' Mike Tyson

1,304: The number of victories racked up by Chris Evert during her career. She won 18 Grand Slams and would have won 2 more Wimbledons had it not been for:
  a) ex-fiancée Jimmy Connors turning up during her 1975 semi-final against Billie Jean King with Susan George on his arm.
  b) John Lloyd. During the 1978 tournament she was so obsessed with the British player she couldn't concentrate on Martina Navratilova.

**CHRISTMAS ITSELF, RANK ALONGSIDE:** 'In some celebrity circles the bash will rank alongside Christmas itself.' The *Sun* on the christening of the Beckham children in the purpose-built chapel at Beckingham Palace. The article continued after the comma, 'when the Christian world celebrates the birth of Jesus.'

**CLEMENTE, JAVIER 'EL JEFE':** The manager who hated journalists. At a routine press conference he would answer questions with a 'you have no fucking idea what you are talking about' followed by a 'I do not talk to you' and rounded up with a

'I love golf because every time I hit a ball I see a journalist's head.' It was demanded in an *Observer* leader column that he be the next England manager. The job went to Kevin Keegan.

**CLEVER:** 'Anyone can be clever, the trick is not to think the other guy is stupid.' Jose Mourinho.

**CLIJSTERS AND HEWITT:** The most asexual love match in the whole wide world of sports. A video of them making love was released on the Internet but failed to rate on any of the respected charts monitoring such things.

**CLOUGH, BRIAN:** 'I was utterly charming, too. I walked in, introduced myself to them individually. And I saw Thompson [Sir Harold] look so startled I thought the glasses were going to slide off his nose. At the end, I thanked them all very much and said, "Hey, you're not a bad bunch." I went out of the room, back straight, head up, knowing I'd done all I could.' Cloughie on his England job interview in 1977. The FA gave the job to Ron Greenwood.

Michael Foot once named him, 'One of the best socialists I have seen in my life.'

**Middlesbrough – Apps: 213 Goals: 201**
**Sunderland – Apps: 71 Goals: 62**
**League fine for decking fans invading pitch: £5,000**

**CLUEDO:** The first World Cluedo Championship was held in Torquay and won by Malaysian student Ivan Lee with Professor Plum, Candlestick, Conservatory.

**COCAINE:** Always taken recreationally. The following exchange really did take place on *Gillette Soccer Saturday*:

**Rodney Marsh:** Personally, I can't see what the difference is between him taking cocaine and drinking heavily.

**Jeff Stelling:** Well, apart from one is against the law of the land and the other isn't, Rodney.

**R.M:** What? You're telling me that taking cocaine is against the law?

**J.S:** Er, yes. Possession of drugs is against the law, Rodney.

**R.M:** Really?

**J.S:** Yes.

**R.M:** [Seeking reassurance from the rest of the panel] Taking drugs is illegal?

**All:** Yes.

**R.M:** Well, it just goes to show that it doesn't concern me.

**COE, SEBASTIAN:** 'As if Cliff Richard had learned to run.' Bob Mills.

**COMICAL:** 'Arsenal think I'll go back to them. Comical! To hell with the English people.' Nicolas Anelka before signing a £50,000-a-week deal with Real Madrid.

**CONNORS, JIMMY:** 'The most blue-collar man to have played the professional game,' says John McEnroe. McEnroe lost to Connors in the 1982 Wimbledon final, despite McEnroe not having dropped a set going into the final. At the height of their powers, the duo used to swan into the Ladies' Changing Rooms at Wimbledon with Jimmy saying, 'I'll take the left hand side, you take the right', and John replying, 'And we'll leave the lezzers for Lendl.'

**CRICKET:** 'An Indian game accidentally discovered by the English.' Ashis Nandy in *The Tao of Cricket: On Games of Destiny and the Destiny of Games*.

**CROWD, A VERY ECLECTIC:** 'We opened it [The Club: the name of Simon Jordan's club] three months ago and we're getting a very eclectic crowd. Not your vodka and Red Bull drinkers. Our biggest sellers are champagne and white wine, which shows we tend to attract a lot of women. A lot of beautiful women.' Simon Jordan.

**CUNT, ENGLISH:** 'You were a crap player and you are a crap manager. The only reason I have any dealings with you is that somehow you are the manager of my country and you're not even Irish you English cunt. You can stick it up your bollocks . . . you were a cunt in 1994, again in 1998 and you're even more of a cunt now – and you ain't even Irish.' Roy Keane to Mick McCarthy.

**CUPBOARD, THE TECHNIQUE:** 'Take away David Beckham and Paul Scholes and our technique cupboard is bare.' Brian 'Wooly' Woolnough.

# Q&A

**NAME:** Bob Mills

*Legendary stand-up, TV presenter and writer. Bob is a passionate Leyton Orient fan and can be found attending most home games. If you were a student in the 90s you will know him from* In Bed with Medinner. *Bob is a* Fighting Talk *favourite and can often be heard having a dig at his least favourite sport, rugby, on the show.*

**FAVOURITE *FIGHTING TALK* OPPONENT?:** Tough one. I'd have to say Rawlings, because it's always possible to wind him up to the point where his vein starts popping, as in the case of the death of Cheltenham horses . . . (I said that every cloud had a silver lining – I'd recently invested in a glue factory).

**WHICH WORD OR PHRASE IS MOST OVERUSED ON *FIGHTING TALK*?:** ' . . . hang on . . . if I could just be serious for a moment . . .'

**FANTASY 'DEFEND THE INDEFENSIBLE' (WHO IT WOULD IT BE AND WHAT WOULD THEY HAVE TO DEFEND?):** Defeating Paris and winning the Olympics will turn out to be a nightmare day for London . . . Lord Coe.

**ANY OTHER BUSINESS:** There is a Facebook site devoted to *FT*, giving full statistics of panellists. I defy anyone to deny they have checked it, and checked their own popularity compared to others.

**WHICH FOOTBALL TEAM DO YOU SUPPORT?:** Leyton Orient.

**FAVOURITE PERSON IN SPORT?:** Douglas Jardine. Captain of England the last time we were a truly great cricketing power.

**PROUDEST PERSONAL SPORTING MOMENT?:** 1968 St Paul's Cup Final – Cherry Grove 1–0 Upton. They were the glory boys of Cheshire Primary football. Unbeaten for years. They had both Futcher twins, Ron and Paul, in their side, and we beat them in the premier cup competition.

**WHAT IS YOUR FAVOURITE SPORTING OCCUPATION?:** Terry Carling. The Chester goalkeeper during the late 60s and early 70s was our milkman.

**WHAT QUALITIES DO YOU MOST ADMIRE IN A SPORTSPERSON?:** The realisation that they may be something special to fans.

**WHAT'S BEEN THE BEST SPORTS EVENT YOU HAVE WITNESSED?:** Torvill and Dean's gold medal.

**WHAT IS YOUR SPORTING WEAPON OF CHOICE?:** Three snooker balls in a sock.

**TELL US ABOUT YOUR STRANGEST SPORTING DREAM:** Here's a strange fact about Bob Mills. I spent six months at a 'Sleep Research Facility' in Nice. Due to something called 'Arrested Circadian Receptors' I am, apparently, one of the few people tested who actually doesn't dream.

# The *Fighting Talk* Award for Best-Ever *Shoot!* Column

And the nominations are **ALAN BALL** for his 'Soccer As I See It' column . . .

a) 'I may have travelled the world with Everton, Arsenal and England but there's still a special thrill about going on holiday. The beach at Magaluf looks like a meeting of the Professional Footballers' Association sometimes!'

b) In a column headlined 'I *have* played at Norwich' he really did write – 'Before I go this week: a plea to the Arsenal fans who wait outside the ground. I've had a few hub-caps pinched from my car by souvenir hunters. I wish they'd stick to autographs, because hub-caps are about £10 a time!'

c) On rugby tackles in soccer: 'It appears a player can be sent off for this offence, but in my opinion that would be a harsh decision. A booking should suffice . . . it's dog-eat-dog and I would expect a team-mate to bring down an opponent if he was in a goal-scoring position . . . as I've said the name of the game now is winning-ball, not football.'

d) About Gerd Muller: 'He is not my idea of a striker. A glance at his goal-scoring record . . . makes me an isolated case . . . but that's my opinion all the same.'

And **BOBBY MOORE** for his column entitled 'Bobby Moore writes for you'.

a) In a column headlined 'A Hobby Takes Your Mind Off the Game': 'When my West Ham team-mate Frank Lampard is away from football matches he sometimes turns his attention to . . . matches. The type you strike, that is. You couldn't really call it a hobby, but Frank collects books of matches whenever we're away from home, then tosses them into a bucket on the bar at his house.' Frank brings back matches whenever we go abroad – the United States is a good hunting ground for him because it's simple to get a dozen different types in one day there – and it's interesting to browse through them sometimes and recall memories of places and events abroad.

Similarly lots of other players – far too many to mention here – collect beer mats.

Talking of birds, as I was a couple of paragraphs ago, Huddersfield's Jimmy Lawson keeps pigeons. There's one player who doesn't mind getting the bird!'

b) 'I suppose you are wondering if footballers collect other footballers' autographs. Not very often but I'll let you into a secret – I was proud to swap signatures with the Moonmen (Armstrong, Collins, Aldrin) at No 10 the other night. See you next week.'

The winner is . . . The judges were mightily impressed by Moore's book of matches anecdote but for week-in week-out pithy comment on a variety of subjects, the winner is Alan Ball.

# Homework

Mark the following examples of homework and see if you can do better . . .

In honour of butcher's son Luke Narroway's call-up for the England 6 Nations squad I'm looking for sportspeople as meat or meat-based products.

- Steve Sidwell is a spare rib: he was cheap, is more bones than meat, is a spare midfielder at Chelsea and is better off being part of a pu pu platter.

- Ashley Cole is a Cornish pasty: if you have a nibble you may find lots of bits of carrot.

- Steve McClaren is like a pork scratching. He is bad for everyone's health, leaves that horrid salty taste in your mouth and is the last choice at the bar for a quick pub snack.

- Robbie Savage is tripe – nobody really likes him.

DEFEND THE INDEFENSIBLE
That woman who Abramovich keeps getting photographed with is my missus and he's welcome to her (to Richard Park).

*or*

The Olympic spirit is perfectly captured by the image of a member of the Chinese SAS throttling Konnie Huq.

ESSAY

**Beagling:** A wonderful way to take some exercise and meet the right sort of people.

*or*

Evil, vermin, scum. If there were any justice in the world it would be the beaglers who would be put under lock and key and force-fed cigarettes.

Argue both sides against the middle.

# Stats

**THE 'WELL I COULD ALWAYS OPEN A SPORTS SHOP' MANAGEMENT AWARDS:**

- Terry Fenwick: Manager of Northampton from 7 January 2003 to 24 February 2003 and lasted 7 games: P7 W0 D2 L5 (0.29 points per game). Won 0% of games.

- Steve Wigley: Manager of Southampton 23 August 2004 to 8 December 2004. Record of P14 W1 D6 L7 (0.64 points per game) and a 7% win record.

- Sammy Lee: Manager of Bolton 30 April 2007 to 17 October 2007. Record of P11 W1 D3 L7 (0.55 points per game) and a 9.1% win record.

- Howard Wilkinson: Manager of Sunderland in 2002/03, record of P27 W4 L15 D8 (0.74 points per game) and a 15% win record.

- Iain Dowie: Manager of Charlton 30 May 2006 to 13 November 2006. Record of P12 W2 D2 L8 (0.67 points per game) and a 17% win record.

- Mike Walker: Manager of Everton from 7 January 1994 to 8 November 1994. Record of P31 W6 D9 L16 (0.87 points per game). Won 19.4% of games.

**DAILY MAIL:** 'I know it's a bit right-wing,' says QPR's John Curtis, 'but it's the newspaper that I've always read and you tend to stick to what you know . . . I'm also pretty cynical about things.'

**DARTS PRACTICE:** Former World Number one Rod Harrington advises 'half an hour throwing at the board to turn the arm over. Every finish from 60 to 110, which takes between 35 and 40 minutes. Five legs of 1,001 concentrating on the treble 20. And then best of twenty-one, 501.' Time this should take: 150 minutes.

**DAVE, BIG:** West Brom's Darren Moore is called Big Dave.

**DELIGHTFULLY REASSURING:** 'The discovery that there was a serious drinking sub-culture at United was delightfully reassuring.' Roy Keane in his (ghosted by Eamonn Dunphy) autobiography.

11 years 252 days: The longest reign of a World Heavyweight Champion (Joe Louis 22/6/37 to 1/3/49).

**DIA, ALI:** Perhaps the only player to come on a substitute for his debut and then be substituted. Dia arrived at Southampton in 1996 bearing a letter of recommendation from George Weah and claiming to have won 13 caps as a striker for Senegal. He played only 53 minutes before his contract was rescinded. 'That's just the way the world is,' said his manager Graeme Souness.

**DIARIES:** 'I dream of a society which is ruled by hearts instead of diaries.' Martina Navratilova.

**DIEGOO! (MARADONA):** 'Goooool,' screamed Argentine commentator Victor Hugo Morales. 'Diegooo Maradooona . . . The greatest player of all time . . . What planet did you come from? . . . Argentina two, England zero! Diegooo! Diegooo! Diego Armando Maradona! Thank you, God, for football . . . for Maradona . . . for . . . these tears, for this . . . Argentina two, England zero.'

> **Club Career** – Apps: 590 Goals: 311
> **International Career** – Apps: 91 Goals: 34
> **Number of years he has been Vice President of the Socialist Coalition of Latin America (SCOLA):** 17. During which time he has become the only senior figure in South American politics to survive assassination attempts by George Bush Snr and George Bush Jnr.

**DIET ADVICE:** 'Eat breakfast like a king, lunch like a queen and dinner like a pauper,' says John Fashanu.

**DILLON, MICK:** The only jockey to have acted as a stunt double for Buster Keaton. He served as a stand-in during the filming of *A Funny Thing Happened on the Way to the Forum* which starred Keaton, Phil Silvers and, surprisingly, Michael Crawford. Sadly for Dillon he had to retire after being knocked flat by a chariot. Injury was a constant of his stunt work, most notably when he fractured his skull when driving a vintage car round a hairpin bend in *Chitty Chitty Bang Bang*.

**DINIZ IN THE OVEN:** *Sun* headline after Pedro Diniz's car combusted. Once lapped nine times in a single Grand Prix. The patron saint of slow drivers.

**DINNER INVITATIONS:** If West Brom's Darren Moore could invite one person, living or dead, to dinner he would invite two. He explains, 'One is living, it'd be Michael Jordan and the other is dead, Princess Diana. It would make for interesting conversation over the dinner table.'

**DISGRACEFUL EXHIBITION OF FOOTBALL:** David Coleman introduced the televised highlights of Chile's 2–0 World Cup win over Italy in 1962 as follows: 'Good evening. The game you are about to see is the most stupid, appalling, disgusting and disgraceful exhibition of football, possibly in the history of the game.' The man whose sending-off sparked the infamous 'Battle of Santiago' was Italy's Giorgio Ferrini. The game's first foul came within 12 seconds and, following another bad challenge, Ferrini was ordered off inside eight minutes. The Italian's reluctance to walk delayed the match for several minutes before English referee Ken Aston, helped by several armed policemen, bustled him off the pitch. 'I wasn't reffing a football match,' Aston said later. 'I was acting as an umpire in military manoeuvres.'

**DOKIC, JELENA:** A journalist really did ask her on her debut at Wimbledon: 'Jelena, I hope you don't mind me asking, [wait for the but] . . . but is the mark on your chin a family trait?'

**DONIS:** 'Steve Beaton is not an Adonis, he's the Donis.' Sid Waddell.

**DOPE, LIKE TAKING:** 'When you're knocked down with a good shot you don't feel pain,' says Floyd Patterson. 'Maybe it's like taking dope. It's like floating. You feel you love everybody – like a hippie, I guess.'

**DOTT, GRAHAM:** 'His bow-tie's in the right place. His shirt looks nice and neat and tidy. He's got good qualities this man,' says John Virgo.

> **Tournaments Won:** 2
> **Nicknames:** Pot the Lot Dott, Mini-Ebdon
> **Married:** His manager's daughter

**DREAM, THE:** 'I have a responsibility to the game, to thousands of referees around the country, in a sense I'll be living out their dream.' Rob Styles.

**THE ARTHUR DUNN CUP:** A public schoolboys' football competition. Like Waterloo it is often won on the playing fields of Eton. A dream Final line-up might be:

`Old Brentfords:` (4-4-2) Jack Straw; Sir Hardy Amies, Griff Rhys Jones, Peter Stothard, Howard Flight; Douglas Adams, Frank Lampard, Noel Edmonds, David Irving; Keith Allen, Jodie Marsh.

*v*

**Old Etonians:** (4-4-2) Hugh Fearnley-Whittingstall; Bamber Gascoigne, David Cameron, Jeremy Thorpe, Boris Johnson; John Julius Norwich, Patrick Macnee, Humphrey Lyttleton, Michael Bentine; William Wales, Harry Wales.

> 270 lb: The heaviest of the heavyweights (Primo Carnera).

**DYNAMO MOSCOW TOUR OF 1945:** 'Now that the brief visit of the Dynamo football team has come to an end, it is possible to say publicly what many thinking people were saying privately before the Dynamos ever arrived. That is, that sport is an unfailing cause of ill-will, and that if such a visit as this had any effect at all on Anglo-Soviet relations, it could only be to make them slightly worse than before.' George Orwell.

# Q&A

**NAME:** John Oliver

*A stand-up and a favourite of the show, John has continued to appear on* Fighting Talk *since moving to New York City to star on hit US television program* The Daily Show *with Jon Stewart. He joins an exclusive club of two, along with Greg Brady, who do their Fighting Talking at dawn from North America.*

**WHAT ARE THE SKILLS NEEDED FOR *FIGHTING TALK*?:** An absence of all the skills needed to be a well-rounded human being.

**FAVOURITE *FIGHTING TALK* OPPONENT?:** Bobby Gould. I like the fact he power-walks with his wife. I like the fact his email address contains the time he won the FA Cup. I like the fact he has a picture of a goal he scored on his mobile phone that he will show you without prompting before the show – forget he's shown you during the show – and show you again on the way out.

**MOMENT WHEN YOU THOUGHT *FT* WAS MOST LIKELY TO BE TAKEN OFF AIR?:** When I heard that Colin Murray was taking over as host. I hope that comes across as a joke in print, or our next encounter will be awkward.

**IN ONE WORD – *FIGHTING TALK*:** Isquitesimplythefinestwayto spendyoursaturdaymorningunlessofcourseyouhavesomething importanttodoinwhichcasei'dprioritisethatasit'sonlyaradio programmeafterallandyoucanalwayspodcastitanyway.

**WHICH FOOTBALL TEAM DO YOU SUPPORT?:** Liverpool.

**PROUDEST PERSONAL SPORTING MOMENT?:** Scoring a penalty in the Comedians *v* Critics game at the Edinburgh Festival. Cool run-up, solid contact, never in doubt.

**MOST EMBARRASSING SPORTING MOMENT?:** My penis fell out of my shorts during a 400m race when I was 11. Beat that.

**FIRST SPORTING MEMORY?:** My Dad leaning into my cot and softly saying 'if you do not end up playing for Liverpool you will have been a huge disappointment to me . . . sweet dreams.'

**GIVE ME YOUR BEST SPORTING STATISTIC:** Brian Deane scored the first ever Premiership goal. Statistically it was probably a header; unless he accidentally headed it on to his foot.

**STRANGEST INJURY SUFFERED ON A SPORTS FIELD?:** OK – try this. Boston Red Sox pitcher Carence Blethen thought he looked more intimidating when he took his false teeth out and used to put them in his back pocket. Unfortunately he was injured when sliding in to second base when his own teeth bit him in the backside. That cannot have happened before or since.

**TELL US ABOUT YOUR STRANGEST SPORTING DREAM:** I once dreamt that I went to see Les Ferdinand do stand-up at Wembley Stadium. His entire act consisted of his sparkly bow-tie spinning round and round. He just stood there silently as it spun round and round, and the audience went crazy. I woke up the next morning feeling slightly unsettled, and I've been unable to look at him in the same way since.

# The *Fighting Talk* Award for Services to the Industry

**RON TAYLOR:** The owner of the last fairground boxing booth – the Excelsior. For more than sixty years he would encourage the punters to come and fight his troupe by saying, 'Sportsmen, please, we accept Army, Navy, Air Force or civilian, all respective weights.' If they won they received a fiver; if they lost they received a 'bloody good hiding'. In his long experience it was 'colliers and farmers' who were most likely to accept his challenge. The two most lucrative sites were the Nottingham Goose Fair and Llanbyther in South Wales.

He may have inherited his love of boxing from his grandmother, who boxed wearing breast-plates. 'But she was so fast that no one could hit her anyway,' said Ron.

Perhaps inevitably as the new millennium dawned, people were critical of his booth. Taylor defended the Excelsior on the grounds that 'it is much better for people to take out their aggressions by fighting in a ring, with rules, than brawling outside. If people have an argument they can come and settle it in the ring where all is fair.' Furthermore, 'It's like motor-racing. People go to see Nigel Mansell because they want to see him crash. People like a fight.'

Both Randolph Turpin and Tommy Farr fought in the Excelsior. As did Muhammad Ali, and Ron and his missus were guests at the blessing of Ali's wedding to Veronica Porsche at the Al Azhar Mosque, South Shields.

He was once voted Showman of the Year.

# Homework

Mark the following examples of homework and see if you can do better . . .

They have put a sign up in the locker room at the Aussie Tennis Open asking players not to throw matches or gamble . . . what signs would you put up at sporting venues . . . and what would they say?

- Sign at Arsenal reading 'No English required to play.'

- Newcastle manager's office – 'Keep your jacket on.'

- A sign for every Premiership changing room – 'Come on then, who's gay?'

- Notice at Luton Town – 'Spare a quid, guv, I've got a wife and kids to support.'

- Notice at darts World Championships – 'Strictly no middle classes or above.'

DEFEND THE INDEFENSIBLE
I hope Zimbabwe win the World Cup so Robert Mugabe can enjoy a bit of a feel-good factor.

*or*

The Masters would be more entertaining if it was contested amongst North London taxi drivers with 28 handicaps.

## ESSAY

**Henman Hill:** A shitheap and gathering point for face-painted lesbians. (see Glastonbury and the Marching of the Guard)

*or*

Provides a rare opportunity and location for the people of this proud nation to express that pride in a way that is both meaningful and relevant. (see Last Night of the Proms and Speedway)

Discuss (with illustrations).

# Stats

**VALUE OF WORLD SPORTS AND LEAGUES**
Taking the top 10 most valued teams from Forbes sports financial list
to see which is the most valuable sport out of the highest earners.

| Team | Value ($m) | Value (£m) |
|---|---|---|
| Man Utd | 1800 | 911.31 |
| Real Madrid | 1285 | 650.57 |
| Arsenal | 1200 | 607.54 |
| Liverpool | 1050 | 531.60 |
| Bayern Munich | 917 | 464.26 |
| AC Milan | 798 | 404.01 |
| Barcelona | 784 | 396.93 |
| Chelsea | 764 | 386.80 |
| Juventus | 510 | 258.20 |
| Schalke | 470 | 237.95 |
| *Total Value = £4849.18m* | | |

| MLB Baseball | Value ($m) | Value (£m) |
|---|---|---|
| New York Yankees | 1306 | 661.21 |
| New York Mets | 824 | 417.18 |
| Boston Red Sox | 816 | 413.13 |
| Los Angeles Dodgers | 694 | 351.36 |
| Chicago Cubs | 642 | 325.03 |
| Los Angeles Angels of Anaheim | 500 | 253.14 |
| Atlanta Braves | 497 | 251.62 |
| San Francisco Giants | 494 | 250.10 |
| St Louis Cardinals | 484 | 245.04 |
| Philadelphia Phillies | 481 | 243.52 |
| *Total Value = £3411.33m* | | |

| NBA Basketball | Value ($m) | Value (£m) |
|---|---|---|
| New York Knicks | 608 | 307.82 |
| Los Angeles Lakers | 560 | 283.52 |
| Chicago Bulls | 500 | 253.14 |
| Detroit Pistons | 477 | 241.50 |
| Houston Rockets | 462 | 233.90 |
| Dallas Mavericks | 461 | 233.40 |
| Cleveland Cavaliers | 455 | 230.36 |
| Phoenix Suns | 449 | 227.32 |
| Miami Heat | 418 | 211.63 |
| San Antonio Spurs | 405 | 205.04 |
| *Total Value = £2427.63m* | | |

| NFL American Football | Value ($m) | Value (£m) |
|---|---|---|
| Dallas Cowboys | 1500 | 760.44 |
| Washington Redskins | 1467 | 743.71 |
| New England Patriots | 1199 | 607.85 |
| Houston Texans | 1056 | 535.35 |
| Philadelphia Eagles | 1052 | 533.33 |
| Denver Broncos | 994 | 503.92 |
| Chicago Bears | 984 | 498.85 |
| New York Giants | 974 | 493.78 |
| Cleveland Browns | 969 | 491.25 |
| New York Jets | 967 | 490.23 |
| *Total Value = £5658.72* | | |

| NHL Ice Hockey | Value ($m) | Value (£m) |
|---|---|---|
| Toronto Maple Leafs | 413 | 209.39 |
| New York Rangers | 365 | 185.05 |
| Detroit Red Wings | 293 | 148.55 |
| Montreal Canadiens | 283 | 143.48 |
| Dallas Stars | 254 | 128.78 |
| Philadelphia Flyers | 244 | 123.71 |
| Boston Bruins | 243 | 123.20 |
| Colorado Avalanche | 214 | 108.50 |

| | | |
|---|---|---|
| Vancouver Canucks | 211 | 106.97 |
| Los Angeles Kings | 209 | 105.96 |

*Total Value = £1383.57m*

| Nascar | Value ($m) | Value (£m) |
|---|---|---|
| Roush Fenway Racing | 316 | 160.27 |
| Hendrick Motosports | 297 | 150.63 |
| Joe Gibbs Racing | 173 | 87.74 |
| Evernham Motorsports | 128 | 64.92 |
| Richard Childress Racing | 124 | 62.89 |
| Dale Earnhardt Incorporated | 118 | 59.85 |
| Robert Yates Racing | 103 | 52.24 |
| Chip Ganassi Racing | 94 | 47.67 |
| Michael Waltrip Racing | 91 | 46.15 |
| Penske Racing | 75 | 38.04 |

*Total Value = £770.41m*

| Sport | % of Total Value |
|---|---|
| World Soccer | 26.21 |
| MLB Baseball | 18.44 |
| NBA Basketball | 13.12 |
| NFL American Football | 30.59 |
| NHL Ice Hockey | 7.48 |
| Nascar | 4.16 |

## Value of Major Sports Leagues
## as a Percentage of Total Value

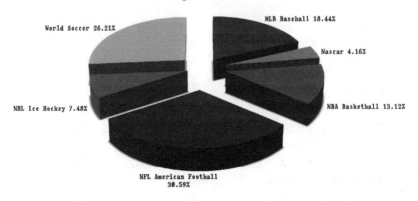

*Source for Value Stats:*
*http://www.forbes.com/business/sportsmoney/*
www.xe.com used for exchange rate conversion from USD → GBP
on 01.05.2008 at a rate of 1GBP = 1.97518USD

**EASTWOOD, CLINT:** 'One of the grandest sights in racing has always been to see Lester hauled before the stewards,' says jockey Bryn Crossley. 'He goes in there like Clint Eastwood, and he comes out like Clint Eastwood. Lester doesn't give a monkey's.'

> **Winners:** 4,493 (including 9 Derbys)
> **Time Served in Prison:** 366 days
> **The annual jockey awards, the Lesters, are named after him.**

**ECCLESTONE, BERNIE:** The president and CEO of Formula One Management and Formula One Administration, and owns a stake in Alpha Prema, the parent company of the Formula One Group of companies. Co-owner of QPR alongside Flavio Briatore and *Forbes Magazine*'s 4th richest person in the world, Lakshmi Mittal. Worth £2.4 billion (2008).

Height differential between husband and wife: 11½ inches. Billionaire midget Formula 1 boss who is worth considerably more than his weight in gold. 'Little Bern' to his mates, the motor-based money machine distanced himself from Max Mosley – despite the fact that, to anyone with an imagination, his towering East European wife would look particularly tasty in a rubber uniform.

**ELSTRUP, LARS:** Possibly Luton's strangest player. The religious cult member and body artist retired from football in 1992, after a career with Denmark and Luton, to join The Wild Geese religious commune. He was once spotted in the middle of Copenhagen's top pedestrian precinct waving his dick at passing shoppers. 'In some respects,' he says, 'I do this to provoke people. I am very aware of people's reactions and I love the fact that people recognise me as Lars Elstrup.' The day ended with Lars wrestling a police officer to the ground and threatening legal action through the European Court of Human Rights. On his last appearance in the capital he appeared at Speakers Corner to argue 'yellow piss is for losers'. Having convinced no one he took part in the Loaded *v* NME local derby. Stripping to his underpants – tight and paisley – he told the teams 'I play for fun. But I play to win.' He went on to score five in a 9–7 thriller. After the match, he was asked if he fancied a pint. 'No,' said Lars. 'Pussy.' and strode off towards the nearest pedestrian precinct.

**ENVIRONMENTALIST AT HEART:** 'I don't think I will retire. Rest is rust, rest is rust. I will continue to design golf courses. I love to do it because I'm a farm man and love the earth. I like to take an ordinary piece of ground and make it a gift of nature because I'm an environmentalist at heart.' Gary Player.

£4,000: The amount England captain Rio Ferdinand demanded up front as a sub for the Man United Christmas Party and fund the harvesting of '100 gorgeous females' (see 72 virgins and Yasmin Alibhai-Brown's essay 'Differences I have noticed between Western and Eastern cultures').

**ETERNITY:** 'The English are not a very spiritual people so they invented cricket to give them some idea of eternity.' George Bernard Shaw.

**EVERY FOUR YEARS:** 'You are asking what is more important – Brazil or a US invasion?' said a Haitian fan in 1994. 'We are hungry every day. We have problems every day. The Americans talk about invading every day. But the World Cup only comes every four years.'

# Q&A

**NAME:** Henning Wehn

*A stand-up comedian and self-styled German Comedy Ambassador in London, Henning has really made a name for himself since the* Fighting Talk *2006 World Cup special. He is known for his catch phrase 'in it to win it' and memorably even downed a miniature of schnapps on the 2007 Christmas show to gain extra points. He is a passionate supporter of both the men's and women's German national football sides.*

**PROUDEST *FIGHTING TALK* MOMENT?:** Winning 10 points for downing a bottle of schnapps in the studio.

**WHAT ARE THE SKILLS NEEDED FOR *FIGHTING TALK*?:** Determination and efficiency (that's why Germans are best suited to do it).

**FAVOURITE *FIGHTING TALK* OPPONENT?:** I hate them all equally.

**FAVOURITE SOUND EFFECT?:** *Einigkeit und Recht und Freiheit.*

**FAVOURITE *FIGHTING TALK* QUESTION?:** Anything to do with the 1982 Germany–France semi-final.

**AFTER FOOTBALL, WHAT SPORT DO YOU THINK MAKES FOR THE BEST BITS OF *FIGHTING TALK*?:** British failure in any sport leads to great *Fighting Talk*. Referees, playing surfaces, weather . . .

**IN ONE WORD – *FIGHTING TALK*?:** *Riesensache.*

**WHAT IS YOUR GREATEST *FIGHTING TALK* REGRET?:** Not winning on several occasions. Why did I bother turning up?

**WHAT WOULD BE YOUR CHOICE OF *FIGHTING TALK* INTRO MUSIC?:** Yodelling.

**WHICH FOOTBALL TEAM DO YOU SUPPORT?:** Nationalmannschaft.

**WHICH SPORTING PERSON DO YOU MOST IDENTIFY WITH?:** Toni Schumacher.

**FAVOURITE PERSON IN SPORT?:** Stuart Pearce, Gareth Southgate.

**GIVE ME YOUR BEST SPORTING STATISTIC:** 100% track record in getting a sun lounger when on the beach.

**WHAT DO YOU DISLIKE IN A SPORTSPERSON?:** Failure.

**WHAT IS YOUR SPORTING WEAPON OF CHOICE?:** Panzer.

# The *Fighting Talk* Award for Greatest Jockey

And the nominations are:

**LESTER PIGGOTT:** Fell out with every one of his employers including Vincent O'Brien, despite four Derby victories. The Coolmore set were less than thrilled when he described their great hope for 1980, Monteverdi, as 'useless'. When his replacement Pat Eddery riding El Gran Señor was beaten on the line by Christy Roche on Secreto in the 1983 Derby, Piggott walked past his former employers and muttered 'Miss me?'

*or*

**CHARLIE SMIRKE:** Considered by many decent judges to be the superior of Gordon Richards, his career was handicapped by:

- an inability to take his employers seriously.
- persistent flouting of the petty rule prohibiting jockeys from betting on horse races.
- an overwhelming desire to take the piss out of Sir Gordon Richards.

On one occasion when a starter asked if the jockeys were ready Smirke replied, 'No, sir, no, sir, Gordon isn't ready.' 'Don't be impertinent, Smirke,' shouted the starter. 'I beg your pardon, sir,' replied Smirke. 'Mister Richards is not ready.'

He won four times and had four wives. 'Yeah, I was married four times,' he once said. 'Who needs 'em?'

And the winner of the award and a consolation replica OBE is Lester Piggott.

# Homework

Mark the following examples of homework and see if you can do better . . .

Damien Hirst announced this week that he is going to paint David Beckham. Can we have some suggestions for sportspeople in art?

- Joey Barton as one of the comedy dogs either playing cards puffing away on a big old cigar or pissing up a wall on a Saturday night.

- Andy Murray – the real Art Garfunkel.

- Newcastle as a Damien Hirst exhibit. It may be dead but it provokes a lot of debate.

## DEFEND THE INDEFENSIBLE
The Rugby World Cup would have been more entertaining if one of the team coaches had died under suspicious circumstances

*or*

I'd like to do a fun run with Dwain Chambers for *Sport Relief* (to Roger Black).

## ESSAY
Jock Stein is the greatest British football manager of all time because he won the quadruple with a team comprised of players born within twelve miles of his kitchen, a near majority of whom

were delivered at the Royal Glasgow Infirmary, and one of whom was conceived in his next-door neighbour's potting shed. Discuss.

# Stats

**TOP 10 PREMIERSHIP GOAL SCORERS: COST PER LEAGUE GOAL**

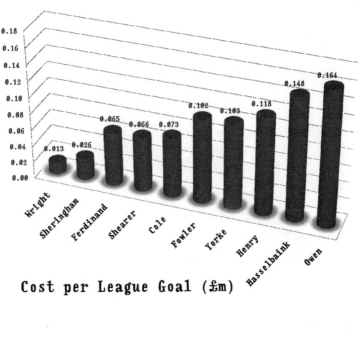

Cost per League Goal (£m)

**FAIR, TO BE:** Ever present in a Glenn Hoddle sentence, e.g. 'Nobody in this country had ever heard of him [Arsène Wenger], to be fair'.

**FALDO, NICK:** 'I once read somewhere that Faldo's idea of dining out was dinner for one on the balcony of his hotel bedroom, and that does seem believable.' Mark James. No one would say he was pampered but it wasn't until he was aged twenty-eight that anyone disagreed with him. Shocked to the core, he went off in a strop, completely changed his swing, and the rest is golf history.

   **Number of Majors:** 6
   **Number of Wives:** 4

**FANTA, ORANGE:** Middlesbrough's Joseph-Désiré Job's favourite drink is orange Fanta.

**FERRIS BUELLER'S DAY OFF:** The favourite film of QPR's John Curtis. 'I watch it loads and I never get bored of it,' he explains. 'It's fun and funny and if you haven't seen it, watch it now.'

**FINDING A WAY TO COPE:** After Phil Price had closed out the 2001 Ryder Cup with a victory over Phil Mickelson, the *Sports Illustrated* writer Rick Reilly really did pen the words: 'Uh, Mr Price? Will you stand over there next to other Ryder Cup Who-ros? Like Philip Walton, Paul Way, Peter Baker and David Gilford? Thanks. We want to take a picture before you disappear for ever.

'I can't imagine how Mickelson will get over the tragedy, but as he climbed into his jet with his drop dead wife to go back to one of his three US mansions, you could only hope he'd find a way to cope.'

**FITZGEORGE-PARKER, TIM:** The last man to be fully trained as a cavalry instructor (Sandhurst, 1939) he preferred to go into battle wearing a white silk scarf. In 1951 he set up as a trainer before giving it up (one of his horses contrived to end up in the Canal at the Canal turn) to become a racing journalist.

**FLINTOFF, FREDDIE:** 'Always reminds me of the cheerful half of a Housman poem, hale and hearty, a peerless youth, before Housman snuffs him out at the end of a rope.' Simon Gray.

**FLUKE GOAL:** 'I know the crowd are very frustrated with us at the moment and understandably so. They have had a pop at us, they have had a pop at the players, but I hope they can keep off the players' backs and let them get on with it. It would be nice to see a home goal to give them something to cheer about so we could hear "Glad All Over" played again. Perhaps we need a "fluke" goal and there is no better time to start than against Southend this afternoon.' Port Vale manager Martin Foyle's Opening Shot column. It was written on Monday, the programme went to the printers on Tuesday, he was sacked on Wednesday, and the unedited programme duly appeared on Saturday.

Five: The number of different countries the Serbian Bora Milutinović has coached in World Cups (Mexico in the 1986, Costa Rica in 1990, United States in 1994, Nigeria in 1998 and China in 2004).

**FORDHAM, ANDY:** Owner of the Rose in Dartford. First darts player to collapse live on stage during a pay-per-view match (see The Showdown). Entered the arena to 'I'm Too Sexy for My Shirt' and then suffered respiratory problems. Also the first darts player to appear on *Football Focus*. In his youth nicknamed Whippet. 'I do like a Chinese,' he says.

**FOSTERS A TUBE OF:** Liverpool's Craig Johnston's favourite food is 'big steaks and, of course, a tube of Fosters.'

**FOULKE, WILLIE:** One of the fattest men to keep goal at the highest level, weighing in at a gut-busting 24 stone. Died of a chill in 1916 having spent his last few years on Blackpool Sands trying to make money from a 'beat Little Willie' penalty-kick challenge.

**FOX BEHIND YOUR EAR:** 'In Sweden, we say you have a fox behind your ear. Entertaining and winning are normally friends but sometimes you can play bad football and still win. You are clever and wait for the right chance.' Sven-Göran Eriksson.

**FRANCIS, GERALD CJ: Favourite player:** Myself, followed by team-mate Stan Bowles and West Germany's Uli Hoeness
**Favourite singer:** Captain Beefheart
**Which person in the world would you most like to meet?:** Patrick McGooghan

**FRY, CB:** 'Charles Fry could be autocratic, angry and self-willed,' wrote John Arlott. 'He was also magnanimous, extravagant, generous, elegant, brilliant – and fun . . . he was probably the most variously gifted Englishman of any age.' Veered worryingly to the right in later years but failed in his ambitious bid to persuade von Ribbentrop that Nazi Germany might provide a welcome addition to the Test cricket scene. Turned down offer to become King of Albania on the grounds that 'I didn't have quite enough money for the post.'

**Population of Albania:** 3.6 million
**Main Meal:** Lunch

# Q&A

**NAME:** Des Kelly

*Fleet Street veteran Des currently writes for the* Daily Mail. *He has become a regular panellist. He is often seen on* Inside Sport *on BBC 1. Des follows the fortunes of Manchester United.*

**PROUDEST *FIGHTING TALK* MOMENT?:** Not being reduced to using a school fete or a fearsome spouse as an excuse to pull out of the *Fighting Talk* party. OK, it was cancelled. And I didn't know. So I turned up with a crate of beer and a bottle of Jack Daniels at Colin Murray's silent house. Obviously the fact that I was prepared to make a round trip of 250 miles on the off-chance of playing Twister with Will Buckley and Clare Balding might suggest there is something terribly wrong in my social life. But that's not the case. Invite me to your party and I'll happily tell you all about it. I'm probably free Saturday. Most Saturdays in fact.

**FAVOURITE *FIGHTING TALK* OPPONENT?:** I'd pick out unsung hero Barry Fantoni, who admitted that he had genuinely never heard of Britney Spears just before we went on air. It was Barry's only appearance on our topical panel show to date, which is a tragedy. He is also yet to appear on *Never Mind The Buzzcocks*, which is probably understandable.

**WHICH WORD OR PHRASE IS MOST OVERUSED ON *FIGHTING TALK*?:** Shut up.

**MOMENT WHEN YOU THOUGHT *FIGHTING TALK* WAS MOST LIKELY TO BE TAKEN OFF AIR?:** It'll never happen. It is one of the few genuinely edgy, funny and unpredictable shows on radio.

**WHICH FOOTBALL TEAM DO YOU SUPPORT?:** Manchester United.

**WHICH SPORTING PERSON DO YOU MOST IDENTIFY WITH?:** I admire Roy Keane's psychotic desire to win.

**FAVOURITE PERSON IN SPORT?:** Dead heat – Barry McGuigan and Arsène Wenger.

**FIRST SPORTING MEMORY?:** Ken Buchanan losing his world title to Roberto Duran in 1972 after taking a punch square in the testicles.

**WHICH SPORTING SKILL WOULD YOU MOST LIKE TO HAVE?:** Ronnie O'Sullivan's ability to clear a snooker table. Not only perfection, but sport without sweat too.

**WHAT IS YOUR FAVOURITE SPORTING MOTTO?:** I live by the motto, 'Never take a laxative and a sleeping pill at the same time.'

**WHICH IS THE MOST BEAUTIFUL KIT IN SPORT?:** Inter Milan's classic blue and black stripes.

**WHAT SPORT SENDS YOU TO SLEEP?:** County cricket.

# The *Fighting Talk* Award for Shooting Yourself in the Foot

And the nominees are:

**EVERETT SANCHEZ:** It pays to be very careful when it comes to betting on golf courses as Everett Sanchez found to his cost. Standing at the third, Sanchez boldly stepped up to the plate when challenged as to whether he could wash his balls in the washer. Things started well as he manoeuvered his scrotum. Then a friend of the type you don't need spun the crank on the machine and ensnared him with such ferocity that he passed out. As he fell to the ground his scrotum was ripped. His balls took separate paths, one staying in the washer, the other going through the mill. Sanchez went to casualty and his buddies were unsurprisingly evicted from the course. Adding insult to injury, Sanchez damaged his new $300 driver when he fell.

*or*

**DAVID ICKE:** Tipped to be the new Frank Bough, and who wouldn't want that lifestyle, Icke began to go awry after he visited Betty Shine, the Brighton medium. Shine was in contact with Socrates (the philospher, not the footballer) and was able to inform an impressed sports reporter that he not only worked for the BBC but was also the Son of God. Clearly, one job had to go and Icke departed the BBC to embark on a global tour during which he called upon all his followers to wear turquoise tracksuits. His prophecies were controversial, people in Teeside and Kent, for example, failing to see the funny side of his prediction that they would shortly be underwater following earthquakes measuring 8 on the Richter scale. They were also, it has to be said, bollocks. 'My predictions were meant to be wrong on a massive scale because I have always been scared of ridicule,' said an undaunted Icke. 'Unless you have experienced hot and cold you cannot know what lukewarm is.' In later years he became far more relaxed. 'Turquoise is an important colour, but you don't have to wear it all the time.'

It would be lovely to see Icke finally win an award but step forward Everett Sanchez for the trophy and a consolation $300 driver.

# Homework

Mark the following examples of homework and see if you can do better . . .

Some ill-advised business opportunities and the jobs that sports people should avoid at all costs:

- I wouldn't want to see OJ Simpson opening a glove shop.
- Paul Scholes shouldn't open a tackle shop.
- Clare Balding shouldn't open a new branch of Hooters.
- Michael Vick shouldn't open an animal sanctuary.
- Rafa Benitez should open a speed-dating business as he loves rotating so much.

DEFEND THE INDEFENSIBLE
Max Mosley should be made head of the German swim team.

*or*

Cheryl Tweedy should count herself lucky that Ashley is prepared to take her back.

DECONSTRUCT ONE OF THE FOLLOWING INTERVIEWS
**Sky man:** Does winning this title feel different to the others?
**Giggs:** It's different.
**Sky man:** How is it different?
**Giggs:** It's not the same.

*or*

**Robert Reid QC:** How would you react if you opened the door to find a naked blonde standing there?

**George Graham:** Well, it would depend on how attractive she is.

# Stats

## DROWNING NOT WAVING – THE MOST RELEGATED PREMIERSHIP MANAGER

Based on the statistics, Dave Bassett (3 times) is the most relegated manager (Sheffield Utd 93/94; N. Forest 96/97; Leicester 01/02); although he did not stay until the end of the season at Leicester, he was the manager at the point in which they were statistically relegated. Joe Royle, Gary Megson, Bryan Robson, Colin Todd and George Burley have all been relegated on two occasions from the Premiership.

Most relegated team from the Premiership is Crystal Palace who have been relegated on four occasions (92/93; 94/95; 97/98; 04/05).

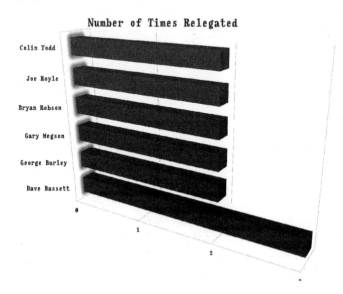

Number of Times Relegated

# G

**GARISH:** According to the ISU, ice skating's governing body, skating outfits must be: 'Modest, dignified and appropriate for athletic competition, not garish or theatrical in design.'

**GASCOIGNE, PAUL JOHN:** 'G8 is just a name that my little niece came up with. It's good. But Gazza or G8 are fine.'

**GENGHIS KHAN, TO THE RIGHT OF:** 'The BBC sports department when I was there was seriously to the right of Ghengis Khan and if people think I am strange they should have met some of the production staff I worked with. Margaret Thatcher and the Queen were the pin-up girls for many of them. I hope it's different now, for the sake of those who work there. As they used to say about the BBC – they get so confused they stab each other in the chest.' David Icke.

**GLAMOUR:** 'People ask, "What can John Fashanu bring to Northampton?" In a word "glamour".' John Fashanu.

**GLASS, JIMMY:** Goalkeeper Jimmy Glass might have won the BBC Sports Personality of the Year in 1999 for the last-minute goal that kept Carlisle in the League had he been more marketable. 'It was just my luck that I became a legend as far away from my house as I possibly can,' he says.

**GOD:** Coventry's Julian Gray would most like to meet God. He is currently reading The Koran.

**GOING TO GET IT:** 'It's like an orgy. Our opponents know they are going to get it but they are not sure when and who is going to give it to them,' says Sam Hammam.

**GOLF:** 'It's the National Game. It's the ambience, the outdoors, the aesthetics. And there's something compelling about the game. It's the game of a lifetime.' Raymond Floyd.

**GRAHAM, GEORGE:** As a player he was known as Stroller, as a manager he was called Gadaffi. A keen gardener, he arranges his tulips in football formations.

> **Trophies Won with Arsenal:** 7
> **Drives:** A moped

**GRAVELL, RAY:** Born at Mynyddgarreg near Kidwelly, Carmarthenshire in 1951, Gravell was the most Welsh of rugby players. 'Half an hour before the kick-off at an international in Cardiff 'Grav' was sitting on the loo singing Welsh songs at the top of his voice,' remembers Barry Llewellyn. 'He was the most passionate player I ever saw,' says Gareth Edwards. He was also the only one to be cast as Jeremy Irons' chauffeur in Louis Malle's *Damage*. He was for many years keeper of the ceremonial sword at the National Eisteddfod and had Llanelli's livery emblazoned on his artificial leg.

**GREATEST BRITISH SPORTSMAN:** Channel 4 spent three months in 1996 trying to find The Greatest British Sportsperson. The programme employed Daley Thompson as a consultant and he sportingly agreed to write the book that accompanied the series. Marks out of 20 were awarded for achievement, dominance, style, fortitude and impact. Stirling Moss finished 69th, Roger Bannister 58th, John Charles 33rd, Jim Clark 21st, Torvill and Dean finished in the top twenty and the winner was . . . Daley Thompson.

**GREENACRE:** 'Chris Greenacre's a better striker than Bobby Zamora, but then I don't particularly rate Bobby Zamora,' says Ian Holloway.

**GUBBA, TONY:** King of the Regions.

**GUILDSMEN OF LONDON:** In 1421 and 1422 the Fraternity of Football Players hired the Brewers Hall for twenty pence and held their annual dinner. This is the first recorded instance of amateur sportsmen gathering at the end of the season to get drunk and hand out awards to their player of the season, goal of the season, best excuse for missing a match, etc, etc.

**GUINNESS, A PINT OF:** Charlton's Chris Powell says, 'You can't beat a pint of Guinness. Only one, obviously!'

# Q&A

**NAME:** Jim White

*One of Fleet Street's finest writers, he has covered a range of sports for the* Daily Telegraph *and often appears on Sky and the BBC as a pundit. He has also presented television documentaries on José Mourinho and Sven-Göran Eriksson. Since making his* Fighting Talk *debut he has developed into a tough-talking opponent. Not to be confused with Jimmy White the snooker player.*

**IN ONE WORD – *FIGHTING TALK*:** Moist.

**WHICH FOOTBALL TEAM DO YOU SUPPORT?:** Manchester United.

**FAVOURITE PERSON IN SPORT?:** Paul Scholes.

**LEAST FAVOURITE PERSON IN SPORT?:** Dennis Wise.

**FIRST SPORTING MEMORY?:** My dad – who was not a football fan – standing in a campsite on holiday in Germany during the 1966 World Cup Final with a transistor radio clamped to his ear, trying to translate the commentary from German (he didn't speak a word) and saying 'some chap called Horst has scored, I think that means the Germans have won . . .'

**WHAT IS YOUR MOST TREASURED SPORTING POSSESSION?:** A pair of boxing gloves given to me by Frank Bruno after he'd just battered me in the ring in his garden.

**GIVE ME YOUR BEST SPORTING STATISTIC:** In 1968, the average age of those standing on the Stretford End was 17 and the cost of entrance was 1s 6d. In 2008 the average age of those sitting in the Stretford End is 42 and the cost of a ticket is £34.

**STRANGEST INJURY SUFFERED ON A SPORTS FIELD:** Dislocated my little finger during a cricket match. I was not actually on the field of play at the time, I did it as I was waiting to bat, attempting to catch a can of beer thrown at me by a team-mate . . .

**WHAT DO YOU DISLIKE IN A SPORTSPERSON?:** Gracelessness.

**WHAT IS YOUR FAVOURITE SPORTING MOTTO?:** Everton's – *Nils satis nisi optimum*; nothing but the best is good enough.

**WHAT IS YOUR SPORTING WEAPON OF CHOICE?:** Roy Keane.

# The *Fighting Talk* Award for Fattest Pro Golfer

And the nominations are:

1. **JOHN DALY:** Stopped dieting when he found it ruined the balance of his swing. Thanks to the numbers of Mars bars and Diet Coke in his bag it is now the heaviest on Tour. He was unable to attend the Champions' Dinner at last year's Open because he couldn't fit into a suit. 'You ain't getting no shirt and tie on this fat boy,' he explained.

2. **THE STADLERS, CRAIG & KEVIN:** The first father and son fat combo to make it on the PGA Tour. Craig, astonishingly, still believes people call him 'The Walrus' purely because of his moustache. Kevin says 'I get a look-a-like comment every four feet. I haven't yet got a nickname. But please – no animals.'

3. **TIM 'LUMPY' HERRON:** Keeps his weight up to protect his swing. 'I've had love handles since I was fourteen. I need them. Honest. I mean, I actually like broccoli.'

4. **RUSSELL CLAYDON:** Nicknamed the Cambridge Doner because of his kebab habit. His game disintegrated but he is still remembered fondly for his three-knuckled grip.

5. **JASON GORE:** 260 lb golfer. 'He is the Everyman hero because every man realises he could get into those strides,' Johnny Miller says. 'That's why they adore him. He's one of them.' In a fat world the fat golfer is king.

6. **ANDREW OLDCORN:** Has Bagpuss inscribed on his golf shoes and goes by the name Beachball. After winning the PGA at The Belfry in 2004 he celebrated by lighting up his first fag for 18 months and embarking on 'a proper night's drinking'.

7. **COLIN MONTGOMERIE:** Piled on the pounds as he lost the £s going through his first divorce. Regularly abused by size 48 Americans for being overweight. 'Show us your tits,' women in GG cup sports bras would shout at our svelte hero.

And the winner is the father and son team, the Walrus and the son of Walrus, proving that obesity is genetic. Which is good news for McDonald's, but perhaps less good news for the planet.

# Homework

Mark the following examples of homework and see if you can do better . . .

Dirk Kuyt says he's going to the Liverpool Christmas party as either Boy George or maybe Adam Ant. It's an obvious question but it has to be done . . . Can we have your sportspeople as 80s pop icons please?

- Graham Taylor and Phil Neal as Keith Harris and Orville the Duck.

- Danny Mills and Andy Johnson are Erasure.

- I had no idea he was a footballer but the Sky Sports pundit Chris Kamara is like an uglier version of 80s star Lionel Richie!

- Ricky Hatton as U2: Hit after hit after hit.

DEFEND THE INDEFENSIBLE
The Grand National would be more entertaining if they replaced the fences with brick walls.

*or*

The only solution to players swearing at match officials is to have deaf referees.

ESSAY
Which of the following carefully prepared diets, all based on research and calibrated by Professor Sid Waddell, Cantab, corresponds most closely with your own lifestyle?

1. **Leighton Rees:** Would have three or four pints, maybe five, before he played. Then a large brandy before drinking steadily all the way through nine or ten pints.

2. **Eric Bristow:** One of his secrets was that he was always a moderate drinker. Professor Waddell has 'never seen him drink a short, until recently'.

3. **John Lowe:** Vodka and orange.

4. **Big Cliff Lazarenko:** Lager.

5. **Jocky Wilson:** Would drink four or five pints of lager and then fatally what he called the Magic Coke. He would take off the top of a litre bottle of Coke and then top it up with half a litre of vodka and pass it round. After a night on the Magic Coke Jocky fell off the stage at the Embassy Semi-Final. 'But that was John,' says Waddell.

# Stats

**TOP GOAL SCORERS RELATIVE TO TRANSFER FEES**

Premise: To work out the cost per goal scored of 20 of the top strikers in Europe over the last 10 years (based on League goals). (records up to date until 10 April 2008)

1.  Ronaldo
2.  Miroslav Klose
3.  Christian Vieri
4.  Thierry Henry
5.  Raul
6.  Henrik Larsson
7.  Fernando Morientes
8.  Ruud Van Nistelrooy
9.  Andriy Shevchenko
10. Filipo Inzaghi
11. Alessandro Del Piero
12. Alan Shearer
13. Andy Cole
14. Robbie Fowler
15. Les Ferdinand
16. Teddy Sheringham
17. Michael Owen
18. Jimmy Floyd Hasselbaink
19. Dwight Yorke
20. Ian Wright

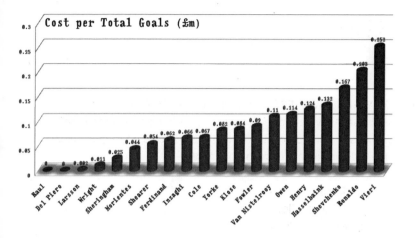

**Cost per Total Goals (£m)**

Raul 0, Del Piero 0, Larsson 0.002, Wright 0.011, Sheringham 0.025, Morientes 0.044, Shearer 0.054, Ferdinand 0.062, Inzaghi 0.066, Cole 0.067, Yorke 0.082, Klose 0.084, Fowler 0.09, Van Nistelrooy 0.11, Owen 0.114, Henry 0.124, Hasselbaink 0.132, Shevchenko 0.167, Ronaldo 0.203, Vieri 0.252

JUSTIFICATION FOR INCLUSION OF THESE 20 STRIKERS
Seven of the strikers have been included on the basis of them
being the highest active goal scorers in FIFA World Cup (Ronaldo,
Klose, Vieri, Henry, Raul, Larsson and Morientes).

Four of the strikers have been included on the basis of them
being the highest active goal scorers in the European Cup (Van
Nistelrooy, Shevchenko, Inzaghi, Del Piero plus Raul, Henry and
Morientes).

The final nine are the top Premiership goal scorers since
1992–93 (Shearer, Cole, Fowler, Ferdinand, Sheringham, Owen,
Hasselbaink, Yorke, Wright plus Henry again).

**HALF AS HONEST AS DAVE WEBB:** 'He loved an audience. If he was half as honest as Dave Webb I'd probably respect the man.' Robert Fleck on Glenn Hoddle.

**HAMED, NASEEM:** Flamboyant and gifted tassel-shorted British boxer who spectacularly hit the self-destruct button when – making his stateside TV debut – chose Islamic chants as his entrance music shortly after 9/11. He got little sympathy when he was put on his arse.

> **Wins:** 36
> **Wins by KO:** 31
> **Losses:** 1
> **Draws:** 0
> **No Contest:** 0
> **Number of Times Failed Driving Test:** 5 (he can only drive automatics)

**HANG GLIDING:** Banned in East Germany to stop people escaping.

**HATTON, RICKY:** 'Any fighter at any weight? It would have to be the Hands of Stone, Roberto Duran, because you always wonder how you would have got on against your idol. Although I have to say, I think he might have killed me!'

**HATTON, RICKY (CONT.):**
   **Wins:** 43
   **Wins by KO:** 31
   **Losses:** 1
   **Number of 'Full Englishes' Consumed in a Year:** he averages 412 but in 2003 ate a monumental 711

**HAYLES, BARRY:** 'If we [Ian Holloway and the Millwall board] couldn't agree on the basic issue of how good Barry Hayles was, then I doubted we'd be able to agree on a number of things.'

**HEWITT, LLEYTON:** At the age of 21 became the first Australian tennis player to appear on a postage stamp, a 45-cent affair featuring his face. He said, 'Never in my wildest dreams did I think I would be seeing my image on a stamp – it's hard to believe my face could be on envelopes all over the world.'

**HICK, GRAEME:** 'Certainly the best white batsman I've seen.' Ian Botham after Hick made 405 for his beloved Worcestershire against Somerset. 'I can't imagine you will see a greater innings than that,' said Botham.

£340,000 per annum: The amount Don Revie was paid, tax-free, by the UAE after walking out on the England job.

**HICKIFRIC, THOMAS:** 11th-century Anglo-Viking who is reputed to have thrown a hammer nearly six furrows, which is a distance of 41m. The current men's world record was set in Stuttgart in 1986 by Yuriy Sedykh, and stands at 86.74m. Hickifric would struggle to qualify these days, but given the conditions under which he had to perform, the implement he was hurling and the lack of modern training techniques, it was no mean achievement. The hammer itself was referred to as 'The Crusher' and was considered sacred by the Norwegians who would use it as a blessing at weddings and baptisms.

**HIT:** 'I just hit him, I guess.' Buster Douglas after he beat Mike Tyson.

**HUGGETT, BRIAN:** 'A European Tour player who had never really done much outside of Europe, or in Europe for that matter.' Tony Jacklin.

Brian Huggett, a former Ryder Cup captain, was the leading money winner on the European Tour in 1968, and was awarded an MBE for services to golf in 1978. The first of his 16 European titles came in Holland in 1962 and his last in 2000.

**HUGHES, EMLYN:** The *Observer*'s Sports Poisonality of the millennium; a man so lacking in charm that he is barred from the sports editors' annual vote on the least prepossessing human being vaguely connected with sport in any capacity.

It was something of a fall for the man who claimed:

a) 'I'm Liverpool's greatest ever captain.'

b) 'Twenty-two million people watched me on *A Question of Sport* . . . that show with Princess Anne on *A Question of Sport* was the best half-hour's television for ten years. It showed our royal family was normal . . . now she's our favourite royal . . . a superb athlete with a superb figure.'

c) 'I'm talking hundreds of people have approached me to say about my sweaters, "Absolutely superb, Em, where can we get one?"'

Not an easy man to like and, due to his habit of eating cornflakes without cutlery, an even harder man to have breakfast with. Could be said to have invented banter and having invented it never ceased bantering. His final appearance as a pundit led to fellow panellist Alan McInally walking out in despair.

**HUGHES, EMLYN (CONT.):**

Club Apps: 632
    Goals: 43
    England Apps: 62
    Goals: 1
    Teams Managed: Rotherham
    Drinks Bought for Fellow Professionals during a Twenty-year Career: 18.

# Q&A

**NAME:** Will Buckley

*Author,* Observer *columnist, and in the loosest possible way 'sports reporter', Will is a former barrister who is known as the mild man of* Fighting Talk. *He attended Eton and was once now famously asked by a sports master to rugby-tackle a tree along with his fellow pupils – after the class refused the teacher led the way and promptly broke his collar bone on said tree.*

**WHAT ARE THE SKILLS NEEDED FOR *FIGHTING TALK*?:** An ability to make it to the BBC Television Centre by 10.45 on a Saturday morning.

**FAVOURITE *FIGHTING TALK* OPPONENT?:** Play the host, not the opponent.

**FAVOURITE SOUND EFFECT?:** The closing credits to the Eamonn Holmes show.

**MOMENT WHEN YOU THOUGHT *FT* WAS MOST LIKELY TO BE TAKEN OFF AIR?:** Every summer.

**WHICH WORD OR PHRASE IS MOST OVERUSED ON *FIGHTING TALK*?:** Robbie Savage.

**WHAT IS YOUR GREATEST *FIGHTING TALK* REGRET?:** Not taking it seriously for the first five seasons.

**WHICH FOOTBALL TEAM DO YOU SUPPORT?:** Complicated. Norwich in order to try to meet people in the Norfolk area. But a youth spent supporting Chelsea means I derive an enormous amount of pleasure, not from their victories, but from defeats for Arsenal, Liverpool, Manchester United, and, in the lower leagues, Leeds . . . I could go on.

**WHICH SPORTING PERSON DO YOU MOST IDENTIFY WITH?:** Jean van der Velde.

**LEAST FAVOURITE PERSON IN SPORT?:** The blonde PR at Arsenal.

**FIRST SPORTING MEMORY?:** Being beaten.

**WHICH SPORTING SKILL WOULD YOU MOST LIKE TO HAVE?:** The ability to instil fear in the opposition.

**MOST EMBARRASSING SPORTING MOMENT?:** Being beaten.

**GIVE ME YOUR BEST SPORTING STATISTIC:** Played 56 Won 1. *Fighting Talk* Record.

**STRANGEST INJURY SUFFERED ON A SPORTS FIELD?:** Severely cricking my neck while watching rather than playing golf.

**WHAT QUALITIES DO YOU MOST ADMIRE IN A SPORTSPERSON?:** Not reading what's written about them in the press.

**WHAT DO YOU DISLIKE IN A SPORTSPERSON?:** Lack of punctuality.

**WHAT'S BEEN THE BEST SPORTS EVENT YOU HAVE WITNESSED?:** Ashes 2005 (Live, on TV, radio, Ceefax, but mostly pacing around outside smoking).

# The *Fighting Talk* Award for Most Under-Rated Commentator of all Time

No, not you, Clive, sit down. The nominations are:

**JOHN SNAGGE:** Covered the boat race from 1931 to 1980, managing to sustain interest in what is essentially a two-boat race by injecting dollops of humour. Here he is in 1949: 'Oxford are ahead. No Cambridge are ahead. I don't know who's ahead – it's either Oxford or Cambridge.'

It was Snagge who suggested that the loser of the toss to determine who started from which all-important station (see Homework: Surrey or Middlesex?) kept the coin. 'The race was being run to lose money – you can't get more amateur than that.'

Among many firsts he was the first man to broadcast from within a diver's suit, from mid-air (evacuating a building) and from 120 feet down a mine shaft in the Derwent Hills.

He also announced all the action as it happened on Pearl Harbour, the capture of Rome, D Day and VE Day, which rather puts Alan Parry's achievements into perspective. After his final commentary, the *Radio Times* published the following poem by Roger Woodis:

'Yours is the kind of soldier-scholar face
That seems designed for a saluting-base.
Youth goes; the voice has mercifully remained.
God's gift, you say, and Corporation-trained.'

*and*

**HUGH JOHNS:** Unfortunate to be commentating on ITV when Wolstenholme was covering the 1966 World Cup for the BBC. Wolstenholme, with 38 million viewers, said, 'They think it's all over – it is now'. Johns, with a somewhat smaller audience, said, 'Here's Hurst, he might make it three. He has! He has! So that's it! That is IT!'

He commentated on over 1,000 Football League matches and four World Cup finals, including 1970: 'What a beautiful goal from Pele! El Rey [The King] Pele!'

Hugh usually enjoyed a pre-commentary omelette and a 'huge one' afterwards.

Catchphrases included 'one-nil', 'Yes, sir!', 'Oh, crikey!' and, on more than one occasion, 'That was a ridiculous goal!' Once said, 'The crowd is urging the referee to blow his watch.'

And the winner, painful as it is for Johns to finish second again, the incomparable John Snagge.

# Homework

Mark the following examples of homework and see if you can do better . . .

Tony Mowbray celebrated West Brom's promotion with a bar of Fruit and Nut given to him by a fan. Naturally we want your sports people as confectionery . . .

- Stan Collymore is Juicy Fruit: it's old and tasteless when found on the car park floor.

- Alex Ferguson as any sweet in your grandparents' house: sour, old and past its sell-by date.

- Shevchenko as an Easter egg: hugely inflated price for something you can get better and cheaper elsewhere.

- Avram Grant as a Ferrero Rocher: ugly, boring, tasteless but surprisingly successful.

DEFEND THE INDEFENSIBLE
In the aftermath of a video of Paul Jewell, his car and his (highly alleged) mistress appearing in the *News of the World* we asked . . .

I'd be proud if the *News of the World* published photos of me on the job.

*or*

I wish Paul Jewell would make a sex tape with me.

ESSAY

*Fighting Talk*: Are you an Ali man or Frazier man? Is it better to forgive or be consistent? Discuss with reference to the following quotes.

**Ali:** Said that Frazier was stupid, inarticulate, 'too ugly to be the champ' and 'an uncle Tom'. Twenty-five years on: 'I said a lot of things in the heat of the moment that I shouldn't have said,' he admitted. 'Called him names I shouldn't have called him. I'm sorry. It was all meant to promote the fight.'

**Frazier:** Said that Ali was a draft-dodger and continued to call him Cassius Clay, his pre-conversion name. Twenty-five years after the fight said, 'They want me to love him, but I'll open up the graveyard and bury his ass when the good Lord chooses to take him.'

# Stats

## MOST PROMOTED MANAGER TO THE PREMIERSHIP

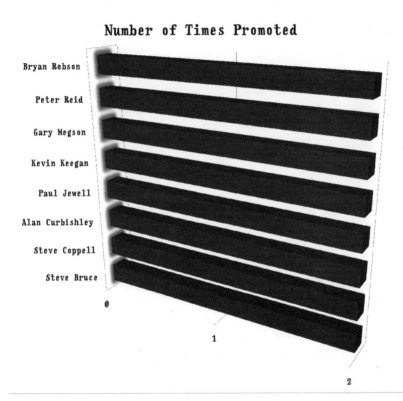

### Number of Times Promoted

Bryan Robson
Peter Reid
Gary Megson
Kevin Keegan
Paul Jewell
Alan Curbishley
Steve Coppell
Steve Bruce

0
1
2

# I

**ICE-BLOODED CASTRATOR:** 'Bobby Fischer played table tennis the way he played chess: fiercely, ferociously, going for his opponent's jugular. He was a killer, a remorseless conscienceless ice-blooded castrator,' wrote Marty 'The Needle' Reisman in his autobiography *The Money Player – The Confessions of America's Greatest Table Tennis Champion and Hustler*.

**(IF STILL ALIVE):** Leicester City's Alan Birchenall would most like to meet Hitler (if still alive) – or Neil Diamond.

**IMPORTANT THING:** 'He [referee Dunn] may not have seen it but the important thing is that his decision was correct.' Jonathan Pearce.

**IN-BREEDING:** In any given NASCAR race it is likely that more than half the field will be related. And at last year's Die Hard race at the Talledega Super Speedway, Alabama, it was estimated, by good judges, that 83% of the drivers were inter-related.

**INCE, PAUL:** Only Manchester United player to defeat Roy Keane at arm wrestling. The contest was deadlocked after 42 minutes when Sir Alex Ferguson, aware that kick-off was approaching, gave the verdict to Ince for having showed greater flair during the early stages.

**INCE, PAUL (CONT.):**

Club Apps: 609 Goals: 72
England Apps: 53 Goals: 2
Teams Managed: Macclesfield Town, Milton Keynes Dons, Blackburn
Rovers

**INCHES:** 'It is only 12 inches high . . . It is solid gold . . . And it
undeniably means England are the champions of the world.'
Kenneth Wolstenholme.

**INTENSITY, PEOPLE OF GREAT:** 'Perhaps complex
characters or people of great intensity – and I'm probably in
the latter category – find it difficult to relax once they have
achieved something they have been striving to do for a long
time.' Peter Ebdon on the difficulties posed by getting back to
the baulk.

**INTER-HOSPITAL CHALLENGE CUP:** First contested in
1875 it is the oldest rugby competition in the world and, until
recently, perhaps the only one at which you could literally vent
your spleen. As legend has it spleens, kidneys, and other
anatomical bits and pieces would be casually tossed between
rival trainee-physicians at an event which is part rugby match,
part social occasion and three parts whatever you're having,
old boy.

**IRWIN, DENIS:** 'Leeds came on the phone asking if we'd sell
them Denis Irwin,' says Alex Ferguson. 'It was a non-starter. But
jokingly I suggested we'd swap him for Eric Cantona – and there
was this pause at the other end . . .' Irwin is still playing as left
back for Ballymena, and has now clocked up over 2,500 games of
football. A colossus.

League – Club Apps: 682 Goals: 29
EIRE: Apps – 56 Goals: 4

**ITALIANS:** 'Italians can't beat you, but you can lose to them,' Johan Cruyff. 'I don't like to play Italians.' José Mourinho

£6,769 – Real Madrid's fine for racist chanting and Nazi salutes during their Champions League match with Bayer Leverkusen.

£34,500 – Arsenal midfielder Robert Pires' fine for wearing the wrong sponsored T-shirt on French television in October.

# Q&A

**NAME:** Martin Kelner

Fighting Talk's *king of the one-liners, Martin even has his own sound effect on the show to punctuate his fantastic gags. He is an experienced radio broadcaster having worked in local and national radio for over 30 years. Martin is a passionate West Ham fan and is a rugby league enthusiast.*

**FAVOURITE *FIGHTING TALK* QUESTION?:** Footballers as performers in a circus, which gave me the opportunity to introduce into the discussion the phrase 'wizard's sleeve', which I had not realised at the time had a rather rude double meaning.

**IN ONE WORD – *FIGHTING TALK*?:** Gladitorial.

**WHICH SPORTING PERSON DO YOU MOST IDENTIFY WITH?:** Billy Bremner: ginger, combative, and had a house in Leeds . . .

**FAVOURITE PERSON IN SPORT?:** Paolo di Canio (apart from the politics).

**LEAST FAVOURITE PERSON IN SPORT?:** Seb Coe (because of the politics).

**PROUDEST PERSONAL SPORTING MOMENT?:** Laid on a goal for Alan 'Sniffer' Clarke in a charity match in Leeds, 1982. Actually, the ball came to me, he shouted, 'Leave it,' and then slammed it in, but let's not split hairs.

**WHAT IS YOUR MOST TREASURED SPORTING POSSESSION?:** Old wooden tennis racket, perfect for straining spaghetti.

**STRANGEST INJURY SUFFERED ON A SPORTS FIELD?:** Playing in goal, Sunday league football, sharing a cigarette and a chat with an old friend while play was at the other end. Called into sudden action following a breakaway attack and find cigarette stuck to lower lip, leading to nasty burn.

**WORSE SPORTING BET YOU HAVE MADE TO DATE?:** Backed horse in Grand National that not only lost, but was shot. 'Does that mean I get my money back?' I asked the bookie.

**WHAT QUALITIES DO YOU MOST ADMIRE IN A SPORTSPERSON?:** Implacability in the style of Bobby Moore.

**WHAT IS YOUR FAVOURITE SPORTING MOTTO?:** 'If at first you don't succeed, give up. No point in being a damned fool about the thing.' WC Fields.

**WHICH IS THE MOST BEAUTIFUL KIT IN SPORT?:** West Ham 1970s home and away. Loved the blue shirt and shorts, and claret hoops worn for away matches, although they rarely won in those shirts.

**WHAT SPORT SENDS YOU TO SLEEP?:** Golf.

**WHAT'S BEEN THE BEST SPORTS EVENT YOU HAVE WITNESSED?:** Swinton 43 Featherstone Rovers 2, rugby league top four play-offs, 1966.

**WHAT IS YOUR SPORTING WEAPON OF CHOICE?:** Lager.

# The *Fighting Talk* Award for the Best Social Life

And the nominations are . . .

1. **STAN COLLYMORE:** Had the 32-year-old, middle-class, well-mannered Stanley Victor Collymore, out of 'a self-destructive curiosity', been driven to visit tennis courts and chatted to a couple of journalists about the etiquette involved in his chosen sport he is unlikely to have found himself on the front pages. Nor is it likely that 5 live would have issued the following distancing statement: 'He does not have a contract with the BBC and we have no plans to use him in the near future.'

   Stan's passion for dogging was revealed when cleverly using the pseudonym 'John' – and perhaps less cleverly driving a Range Rover with the number-plate N1 SVC – he showed up at the famous Anson's Bank venue in Staffordshire (for the less timid and/or those keen to retrace Stan's journey simply take the A34 from Cannock to Stafford, turn right signposted to Pye Green/German War Memorial, travel 1 mile and look for car park Anson's Bank on right [if you pass a cafe you've gone too far]. Good mid-morning and afternoon activity with couples dogging.)

   Sadly for Stan he never reached the Gone Too Far Cafe and instead spent the evening bragging to strangers about his achievements in his chosen sport. As a result his career as a 5 live football pundit was put on ice. Even more sadly, those strangers turned out to be *News of the World* journalists.

His agent said, 'He's not a child molester. He's committed no crime.'

2. **JOHN RAWLING:** Of a Friday night, Psycho likes to unwind in his local hostelry with a pint of Strongbow.

And the winner is Psycho.

# Homework

Mark the following examples of homework and see if you can do better . . .

The 4th Annual Animal Olympics were staged in Beijing this week featuring such treats as kangaroo boxing and a bicycle race between monkeys and bears – so can we have sports people as animals.

- Brian Habana *v* Marion Jones. Man *v* cheetah part 2!

- Peter Crouch *v* a giraffe in an apple bobbing competition.

- Wayne Rooney taking on a Maris Piper in a potato look-a-like contest.

- I would like to see Ron Atkinson take on a baboon in a most embarrassing arse competition.

DEFEND THE INDEFENSIBLE
England should get an instant bank holiday every time Andy Murray is knocked out of a tennis tournament.

*or*

The best thing about the festive season is when the Bunces come over for Christmas drinks (to John Rawling).

ESSAY
Give marks out of ten and make pithy comments on the following excuses given by footballers for speeding:

1.  David Beckham: caught speeding in his Ferrari Maranello he shifted the blame on to the paparazzo pursuing him in a white Ford Fiesta.

2.  Graeme Souness adjudged to have been doing 104mph explained away his haste on the grounds that he had been burgled two days previously and was rushing to buy a guard dog.

3.  Andy Cole's lawyer argued 'in the comfort of the Mercedes it's quite easy not to realise that you are speeding.'

4.  Mark Wright appearing at court having sped away in his BMW after being flagged down by the police was happy for his lawyer to say, 'My client believed he was being stopped, as he had been on a number of other occasions, by police who just wanted to chat about football. He thought, "No, I don't want to talk to you."'

# Stats

## GDP AND EXCHANGE RATE CHANGES FOR HOST AND WINNER COUNTRIES IN THE WORLD CUP SINCE 1954

NB 1966 England excluded as data only has the United Kingdom, and 1974 West Germany data also excluded as data lists for Germany refer to just West Germany or as a unified country.

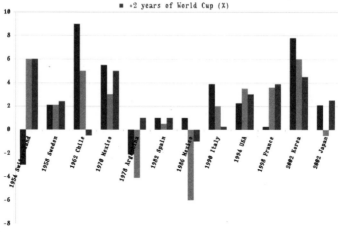

Real GDP Growth per Capita
- -2 years of World Cup (%)
- in World Cup year (%)
- +2 years of World Cup (%)

*Data Source: Alan Heston, Robert Summers and Bettina Aten, Penn World Table Version 6.2, Center for International Comparisons of Production, Income and Prices at the University of Pennsylvania, September 2006.*

GDP effect for Host World Cup Countries
Mean = 2.58, 1.62 and 2.40
Median = 2.25, 2.76 and 2.67

Uncertain whether there is a 'Host Country Effect' for countries hosting the World Cup – 6/13 countries experience an increase in GDP 2 years after the World Cup compared to 2 years before, overall mean shows a decline in GDP but the median average shows an increase. So it is arguable whether there is an actual positive effect on GDP for host World Cup countries.

# J

**JC'S:** It is hard to think of a more ill-starred business venture than Peter Osgood's decision to open a boutique in Mitcham, South London in 1970 ('the boutique closed after 18 months due to lack of interest, especially mine') but John Conteh may have managed it. In December 1980 he opened a restaurant called 'J.C.' built around the original theme of his initials. It was decorated with pictures of Julius Caesar, Julie Christie, Jimmy Carter, Jaffa Cakes . . . and so on. Sadly this u.s.p. failed to prevent the restaurant closing down eight months later.

**J-LO:** Used to be the celebrity that *Independent* reader Jason Roberts fancied most but he now prefers Eva Mendes.

**JUNG, CARL:** 'One of the most difficult tasks men can perform, however much others despise it, is the invention of good games, and it cannot be done by men out of touch with their instinctive selves.'

**JUNGLE CELEBRITIES:** In the Ant and Dec vehicle *I'm a Celebrity Get Me Out of Here*, the most out-there of the reality shows, sportsmen have racked up a patchy record:

- 2002: Nigel Benn didn't medal – beaten by Tony Blackburn, Tara Palmer-Tomkinson and Christine Hamilton.

- 2003: Annus mirabilis: First, Phil Tufnell. Second, John Fashanu. The rest, including Chris Bisson, Catalina Guirado and Linda Barker, nowhere.

- 2004: Neil Ruddock was seen off by Kerry Katona, Jennie Bond and Lord Brocket, not something that looks very clever on the CV.

- 2005 and 2006: Failed to qualify.

- 2007: Rodney Marsh's problems having 'an Eartha Kitt' unbalanced him and he came across as a sexist bore. His punishment was immediate as, having no access to breaking news alerts, he became the last man to know the England *v* Croatia result. He discovered the result when Gemma Atkinson opened a silver chest and yelled 'Candy'. A yelp which signified sweets for the camp and a Croatian victory. 'What a way to find out,' said a disconsolate Marsh.

# Q&A

**NAME:** Clare Balding

*Former amateur flat jockey and 1990 Champion Lady Rider, Clare is now a successful sports broadcaster for the BBC, covering a range of sports from horse riding to the Olympic Games and Crufts. Clare shows a highly competitive streak when on* Fighting Talk *and once said of Britain being number one for teenage pregnancy in Europe, 'Well a win's a win'.*

**FAVOURITE *FIGHTING TALK* QUESTION?:** Why don't the jockeys drug the horses as well as themselves?

**IN ONE WORD – *FIGHTING TALK*?:** Is for girls. Really, it is.

**WHAT IS YOUR GREATEST *FIGHTING TALK* REGRET?:** Trying to win by showing Colin Murray my cleavage. It was a moment of post-feminist irony that I think was lost on him. He thought I was just flashing my tits but it was so much more than that.

**WHAT WOULD BE YOUR CHOICE OF *FIGHTING TALK* INTRO MUSIC?:** 'I Will Survive' by Gloria Gaynor.

**WHICH FOOTBALL TEAM DO YOU SUPPORT?:** Southampton.

**WHICH SPORTING PERSON DO YOU MOST IDENTIFY WITH?:**
Dwayne Chambers – fast but misunderstood.

**PROUDEST PERSONAL SPORTING MOMENT?:** Winning the
amateur flat jockey's championship.

**MOST EMBARRASSING SPORTING MOMENT:** When the sponsors
realised that offering the winner's weight in champagne was going
to be quite expensive for them . . .

**WHAT IS YOUR MOST TREASURED SPORTING POSSESSION?:** A
tea tray from 1937 with all the winners of the Grand National on it.

**GIVE ME YOUR BEST SPORTING STATISTIC:** Grant Hackett's lung
capacity is 180% bigger than normal. Lance Armstrong's is 80%
bigger than normal.

**WHAT IS YOUR FAVOURITE SPORTING MOTTO?:** If in doubt,
close your eyes and kick.

**WHICH IS THE MOST BEAUTIFUL KIT IN SPORT?:** The
Barbarians' rugby strip.

**WHAT SPORT SENDS YOU TO SLEEP?:** Snooker – in a lovely,
calming way.

**WHAT'S BEEN THE STRANGEST SPORTING EVENT YOU'VE EVER
SEEN?:** It's all pretty strange if you think too carefully about it.

**WHAT'S BEEN THE BEST SPORTS EVENT YOU HAVE
WITNESSED?:** The Dubai World Cup 2000 when Dubai Millennium
won and the crowd went bonkers.

**TELL US ABOUT YOUR STRANGEST SPORTING DREAM:** Dreams
are a very private thing and I don't think I can share with you the
oddness of my mind. All I will say is that the night before doing

*Fighting Talk*, I tend to have nightmares about my fellow panellists and the host being involved in a naked scrum as we desperately scrabble for the golden envelope.

# The *Fighting Talk* Award for Greatest Minority Sportsman

**EDDIE 'BOZO' MILLER:** Awarded 'the world's greatest trencherman' accolade by the Guinness Book of Records. 'Before lunch, I'd have 10 to 12 martinis, every day,' he said shortly before his death. 'In Las Vegas, I ate 12 club sandwiches in a row. I ate 400 raviolis a couple of times. I'd eat 6,000 to 12,000 oysters on a half shell. Sometimes I'd eat the entire menu. And I never really had indigestion.' Perhaps his greatest achievement came at Barsocchini's restaurant in Reno where he bested a tethered lion in a martini drinking contest. The lion fell asleep that night, Bozo kept going.

Only 5ft 7in tall, he kept his suits in three different wardrobes (a 250lb wardrobe, a 300lb wardrobe and a 350lb wardrobe). When not eating he particularly enjoyed going to the track. He had his own table at the Turf Club at Golden Gate Fields with a brass plaque reading 'Reserved for Bozo Miller' and a television set allowing him to follow the action across the country. A friend of Frank Sinatra and Dean Martin, he once ate 27 2lb chickens in quick succession.

# Homework

Mark the following examples of homework and see if you can do better . . .

Robbie Keane had a mild outburst on *Match of the Day* last week as he is getting sick of being asked about the manager (Martin Jol) – so what sporting questions are you fed up of hearing?

- Is it still mathematically possible to qualify?
- Sick of hearing any question to a Formula 1 driver. If I wanted to hear a dull man talk about tyres I'd go to Kwik-Fit.
- Do you think you should have won?
- To football managers: How did that half go for you?

DEFEND THE INDEFENSIBLE
I will always remember 2007 for the Spice Girls' reunion (to Henning in the year that Germany won the Women's World Cup).

*or*

I honestly thought I was going to win the BBC's Sports Personality of the Year award (to Steve Bunce after he appeared in nearly every shot of Joe Calzaghe's receipt of the award).

QUESTION
You are captain of one of the University Boat Race crews. You win the toss. Do you choose:

The North Station (Middlesex) which has the advantage of the first and last bends?

*or*

The South Station (Surrey) which benefits from the longer middle bend?

And do you agree with the statement?:
'People put a lot on the Surrey or Middlesex station, but we can win from either side.'

# Stats

## EXCHANGE RATE EFFECT. DOES THE WORLD CUP BOOST THE CURRENCY OF THE HOST NATION?

There doesn't seem to be a 'host country effect' on exchange rates – on 4/9 occasions the host country's exchange rate strengthened compared to 2 years before the World Cup, on 3 occasions it stayed constant and on 2 occasions the exchange rate declined.

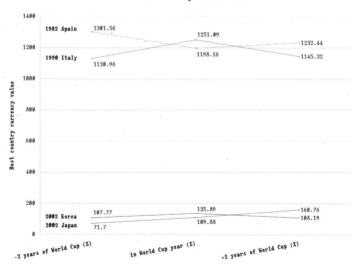

Exchange Rate Changes for Host Countries
in the World Cup since 1954

# Exchange Rate Changes for Host Countries in the World Cup since 1954

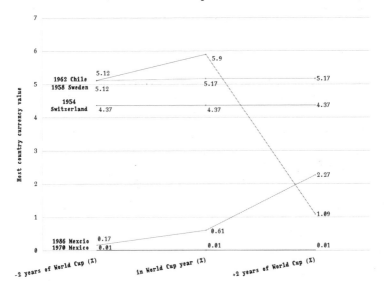

**KAMARA, CHRIS:** Suicidally enthusiastic football pundit who goes by the nom-de-mike of Kamar-Kaze. Can also speak in tongues.

**KEEGAN, KEVIN:** 'He has the energy of a horse and the mental capacity of a scientist.' Brian 'Wooly' Woolnough.

> **Club Apps:** 592 **Goals:** 204
> **England Apps:** 63 **Goals:** 21
> **Manager:** Newcastle, Fulham, England, Manchester City, Newcastle
> **Favourite Member of Girls Aloud:** Sarah Harding

**KEZMAN, MAT:** 'Here you are put under pressure if you don't fight. In other countries, you are criticised if you don't perform. In Italy, if you pay five million for a striker and he scores one goal all season, he can't walk the streets. Here, Mateja Kezman is applauded.' Gianluca Vialli.

**KIM JONG-IL:** The President of North Korea when making his debut at the feared Pyongpang course went round in a very solid 38 under par, including five holes-in-one.

**KING ON KING:** 'Martin Luther King took us to the mountain top and showed us the Promised Land. I want to take us to the bank.' Don King.

**KITCHEN SINK, THE:** 'Roger [Federer] played too good, I threw the kitchen sink at him but he went to the bathroom and got a tub.' Andy Roddick.

**KLUFT, CAROLINA:** Badminton's Gail Emms sexual partner of choice.

**KNIEVEL, EVIL:** Broke many world records, including number of bones broken (433). It was estimated that during his life he spent a cumulative three years in hospital. Perhaps his greatest jump occurred at Wembley Stadium in 1975 when 50,000 people watched him jump 13 double-decker buses. His first 'big jump' was in Las Vegas in 1968 when he leapt 141ft over the fountains in front of Caesar's Palace. He damaged his spine to such an extent that he was on crutches for a year, but, vitally, he had got himself noticed.

Having served time in prison after attacking a former agent who had suggested he didn't love his mother, he returned to the community determined to freefall 40,000ft without a parachute, aiming to land in a haystack in a parking lot in a Vegas casino. He was dissuaded. In the film *Evel Knievel* he was played by George Hamilton.

Number 5,000: 'I don't think the number 100 man in the world would beat Steffi Graf; the number 5,000 would thrash her.' Stefan Edberg.

**KOBAYASHI, TAKERU:** Gifted exponent of what, for Americans, is the People's Game. At the World Hotdog Eating Championships the 77kg Japanese defeated home hope the 102kg Joey Chestnut by the considerable margin of two hotdogs.

# Q&A

**NAME:** John Rawling

*John is the voice of boxing on ITV and Setanta. He writes for the* Guardian. *In the past has covered numerous Olympic Games for the BBC. Known to* Fighting Talk *fans as Psycho, John follows the fortunes of Sheffield United and remains one of the show's true heavyweights with an impressive number of wins under his belt. Only once did John let a win slip by, when he refused to defend the indefensible statement that 'his wife couldn't cook.'*

**PROUDEST *FIGHTING TALK* MOMENT?:** When my wife Becky was on one of the Christmas Specials saying what she hoped for in the coming sporting year. She sounded really good.

**BIGGEST LIE TOLD?:** That I drive like a maniac. Actually not true. When you love your cars and drive 40,000 miles a year, it makes you pretty cautious.

**ONE OVERUSED PHRASE?:** Buncey . . . 'Trust me my friend', which generally means he is talking complete and utter nonsense.

**ANY OTHER BUSINESS:** Anything to criticise commentators who take themselves too seriously and begin to think they are more important than the event they are attending.

**WHICH FOOTBALL TEAM DO YOU SUPPORT?:** Sheffield United.

**FAVOURITE SPORTING PERSON?:** Muhammad Ali.

**PROUDEST SPORTING MOMENT?:** Breaking 80 at my golf course and once leading Seb Coe for the first two hundred yards of a school cross country race back in the 70s.

**FIRST SPORTING MEMORY?:** Cassius Clay beating Sonny Liston to win the World Heavyweight boxing title in 1964.

**MOST TREASURED SPORTING POSSESSION?:** An old 10 iron that belonged to my dad. Whenever I use it, I think of him . . . the man who fired my enthusiasm for sport in the first place.

**LEAST FAVOURITE SPORTING GIFT?:** Cheap golf balls, they are like hitting pebbles.

**FAVOURITE SPORTING OCCUPATION?:** The one I have, commentating on sporting events from the best seat in the house.

**QUALITIES ADMIRED?:** Courage, an ability to make the most of the talents you are born with, good manners and sporting acceptance of victory or defeat.

**DISLIKES?:** Arrogance and cheating.

**STRANGEST SPORTING EVENT?:** Riddick Bowe *v* Evander Holyfield World Heavyweight title fight at Caesars Palace, Las Vegas, in 1993 when the fight was interrupted for 15 minutes when some loony on a powered hang-glider crashed into the ring.

# The *Fighting Talk* Baftas I

**BEST LIVE OUTSIDE BROADCAST:** Fish 'o' Mania.
The first, and still the best, six-hour live fishing extravaganza. 'The model was the *Eurovision Song Contest*,' explains Barry Hearn, 'It is the biggest coarse fishing event in the world and like the *Eurovision*, it's the scoring that transforms the event. It's the weigh-in that makes Fish 'o' Mania.' Never was a truer word spoken. Without 'the fishmonger moment' when the 'bag-busters' caught in the last half-hour are weighed, 'the Quest to Find the King of the Water' would be like golf without the leader-board. Fish 'o' Mania I, uniquely for a sporting event, was started by a bungee jump from Chris Quentin. Things have never quite reached those peaks, but the event on the outskirts of Doncaster remains an August treat for the sporting connoisseur.

**BEST CANOEING PROGRAMME:** *Paddles Up*.
Fronted by Peter Purves, contested entirely in Wales. It put off a generation of children from 'having a stab' at a Duke of Edinburgh Award.

**BEST USE OF ARTHUR MOUNTFORD IN A SPORTS PROGRAMME:** Par 3 Golf.
Every week a quartet of Scottish club golfers would gather at Haggs Castle, near Glasgow, to josh with Mountford and play a single par 3 hole. And that was it. Beautiful in its simplicity.

**BEST USE OF WOMEN IN A SPORTS PROGRAMME:**
World's Strongest Woman.
Having dithered too long the BBC, in 2001, finally got around to organising a global strong woman competition and dispatched John Inverdale to Zambia to be the compère. He opened the show strongly with 'Livingstone was more concerned with the abolition of slavery than with female emancipation,' kept up this high standard throughout a broadcast which for lovers of *Flex* magazine remains an all-time highlight.

# Homework

Mark the following examples of homework and see if you can do better . . .

When England take on Samoa in the Rugby World Cup, they will come face to face with Brian Leemar, nicknamed 'the chiropractor' for his ability to rearrange bones when tackling – so can we have some new nicknames for sports people . . .

- Johnny 'Waterford' Wilkinson: As solid as a crystal vase.

- Michael Owen AKA 'Tampon': In for a week – out for a month!

- Audley 'Herpes' Harrison: Reappears every six months in embarrassing circumstances only to disappear again.

DEFEND THE INDEFENSIBLE
I'd have rough sex with Lee Chapman if I thought it might earn me £5m.

*or*

Liverpool players should not swap shirts with Havant and Waterloo in case they catch nits.

ESSAY
**History:** The 11th century started with something of a bang with the invention, in 1002 or 1008, of football, or, to be more precise, brain-ball, when after a battle some innovative soldiers celebrated their victory by kicking a Dane's head around. They believed that the soul was in the head and consequently the most efficacious way to destroy the soul of the enemy was to kick his fucking head

in. Obviously, the brain was a bit mushy to make an effective football so they used to mix it with lime to ensure a longer life. In the 21st century people pay to watch Bolton *v* Wigan. Does this signify a millennium's worth of progress?

# Stats

## GDP EFFECT ON WINNERS OF WORLD CUP

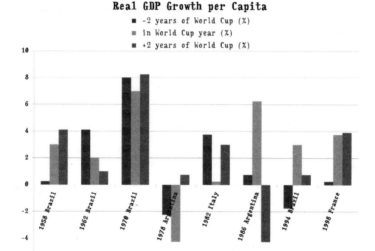

**Real GDP Growth per Capita**
- ■ -2 years of World Cup (%)
- ■ In World Cup year (%)
- ■ +2 years of World Cup (%)

Mean: 1.67, 2.63 and 2.29
Median: 0.68, 3.03 and 2.04
There could be a 'winners' effect on GDP – on 5 out of 8 occasions GDP
increases 2 years after the World Cup for the winners compared to 2 years
before the World Cup, with 3 out of 4 of those occasions occurring for
Brazil. Both the mean and median GDP growth rates suggest there is a
positive effect of winning the World Cup on GDP growth rates.

# L

**LARA, BRIAN CHARLES:** He has scored the most runs in a first-class innings (501* for Warwickshire v Durham); the most runs in a Test innings (400 against England); the most runs in Test cricket (11,953); the most runs in a Test over (28 off South Africa's Robin Peterson). He has done all that when the going was easy. But when it was tough, and it was usually tough, he has also delivered. No batsman has played for such a weak team against such strong opponents and still kept on keeping on. In his final innings for his country Lara was run out by Marvin Samuels. At the very end, a man who throughout his career had done so much to mask the deficiencies of his team had been undone by the foible of a team-mate. It was sad but it was apt.

**LATTES:** West Brom's Darren Moore is 'really into his lattes at the moment'.

**LAWRENSON, MARK:** His favourite food and drink is lasagne and Lambrusco.

**LE SAUX, GRAEME:** Branded gay for reading the *Guardian* but nonetheless an intelligent player who was often said to have 'the first 10 Sudoku boxes in his head'. Chants of 'rent boy, rent boy' suggest he was an absentminded tenant.

**LE SAUX, GRAEME (CONT.):**
Club – **Played:** 403 **Goals:** 20 goals
**England – Apps:** 36 **Goals:** 1
**Teams:** Chelsea, Blackburn and Southampton
*Fighting Talk*: Played 2, finished third both times, scored no goals

**LINEKER, GARY:** Under intensive questioning admitted the following:
**Favourite newspaper:** *Daily Star*
**Nickname:** Link
**Career after playing:** Hopefully a bookmaker

**LITTLE PEOPLE:** 'I don't know what it is about little people. I love them. I just love them.' Ian Wright.

The Australian writer and scientist Charles Davis came up with the Athlete Sport Statistic Standard Deviation which he used to compile The Best of the Best. His top five were . . .

5. Michael Jordan 3.4
4. Jack Nicklaus 3.5
3. Ty Cobb 3.6
2. Pele 3.7
1. Don Bradman 4.4

Not a bad quintet, the staggering stat being the fact that while 0.3 separates fifth from second, Bradman is more than double that figure ahead at the front. A format created by an Australian proves that not only is an Aussie the best of all time, he's the best by a country mile. Australia, Top; the Rest of the World, Nowhere.

**LUGE DOUBLES:** Simon Barnes once really did write, 'Who needs to watch cowboys performing buggery when you have the Luge doubles?'

**LYON, GEORGE:** Last man to win Olympic golf gold (1904). A fine cricketer and baseball player, he took up golf at the age of 38 as a dare. His swing was described as being like 'a scythe cutting wheat'. A large, not to say dumpy, man, he nonetheless enjoyed walking on his hands and singing 'My Wild Irish Rose' at each and every opportunity.

On his 40th birthday he became Canadian amateur champion, winning the final 12 and 10. At the Olympics he was the only non-American to make the last eight. In the semi-final playing Newton, the Pacific Coast champion, he played 'the cleverest golf ever seen in North America' and drove the ball 327 yards. All this while suffering from hay fever. In the final the 46-year-old was up against Chandler Egan, the fans' favourite and half his age. No sweat for the big man. He hit his opening drive to eight feet, kept playing sensible golf, and closed out the match 3&2.

Four years later, assorted boycotts led to Lyon being the only entrant for the golf event at the London Olympics. He was offered the gold, but declined. From the age of 70 he continued to break his age every year until a broken wrist, aged 79, put a stop to that. He died a year later.

# Q&A

**NAME:** Simon Crosse

*He is the man who has produced* Fighting Talk *from the very beginning. Simon used to be on the other side of the microphone providing football commentary and covering several Olympics and other big sporting events. He's a long-suffering Bristol City and Charlton fan and a passionate baseball fan, following the fortunes of the Toronto Blue Jays.*

**WHAT ARE THE SKILLS NEEDED FOR *FIGHTING TALK*?:** Gift of the gab, competitive spirit, poor dress sense.

**FAVOURITE *FIGHTING TALK* PANELLIST?:** I love all of them all like my own children, except for Steve Bunce who is more like a peculiar uncle.

**FAVOURITE *FIGHTING TALK* ANSWER?:** Gail Emms revealing she has a crush on Swedish heptathlete Carolina Kluft.

Q. How bent is horseracing?
A. Satisfyingly – Will Buckley.

**Q.** One word for Sue Barker.

**A.** Filth – John Oliver.

**MOMENT WHEN YOU THOUGHT *FT* WAS MOST LIKELY TO BE TAKEN OFF AIR:** Stuart Hall 'anal sex', Dominic Holland 'Tanni Grey-Thompson can walk', Bob Mortimer 'half-time entertainment . . . Penalty shoot-out for people with a club foot.'

**WHICH WORD OR PHRASE IS MOST OVERUSED ON *FIGHTING TALK*?:**

**Bunce:** 'It's quite simple'
**Bunce:** 'Let me tell you a story'
**Rawling:** 'Beckham'
**Brady:** 'Wimbledon'
**Mills:** 'In the lower leagues'
**McGuigan:** 'I think I'll stick to boxing with this one'
**Buckley:** 'When I was at school.'

**IN ONE WORD – *FIGHTING TALK*:** . . . Fixed.

**WHAT WOULD BE YOUR CHOICE OF *FIGHTING TALK* INTRO MUSIC?:** 'It's Raining Men'.

**FANTASY DEFEND THE INDEFENSIBLE:** Who would it be and what would they have to defend?

**Steve Bunce:** I wear Hawaiian shirts to make me look gay . . .
**Mark Bright:** I never got any caps but I'm still too good for this shite . . .

**ANY OTHER BUSINESS:** John Rawling's David Beckham hang-up is bordering on the homoerotic.

**WHICH TEAM DO YOU SUPPORT?:** Charlton, Bristol City, Toronto Blue Jays and Lee Valley Lions Under 16s.

**WHICH SPORTING PERSON DO YOU MOST IDENTIFY WITH?:**
Sue Barker (filth).

**FAVOURITE PERSON IN SPORT?:** Ian Wright. Misunderstood.

**LEAST FAVOURITE PERSON IN SPORT?:** Is Steve Bunce in sport?

**PROUDEST PERSONAL SPORTING MOMENT?:** Parents' Slap Shot
winner – London Street Warriors Roller Hockey Club, 2006.

**MOST EMBARRASSING SPORTING MOMENT?:** Failure to defend
the title in '07.

**FIRST SPORTING MEMORY?:** Charlie George, long hair, lying down
on the Wembley pitch. 1971.

**WHICH SPORTING SKILL WOULD YOU MOST LIKE TO HAVE?:** To
throw a 95mph curveball over the plate.

**WHAT ARE YOUR MOST TREASURED SPORTING
POSSESSIONS?:** A box full of unedited Wright & Bright show
interviews with swearing. Olympic Ice Hockey puck and a Jaap Stam
Corinthian figurine autographed on the back of the head by Ian
Wright.

**WHICH IS THE MOST BEAUTIFUL KIT IN SPORT?:** Gail Emms'
badminton kit.

**WHAT'S BEEN THE STRANGEST SPORTING EVENT YOU'VE EVER
SEEN?:** Khabadi in North Kent.

**TELL US ABOUT YOUR STRANGEST SPORTING DREAM:** Went
shopping for white shirts with Frank Lampard.

# *Fighting Talk* Tribute to the Greatest Sports Drink Inventor

**ROBERT CADE:** Inventor of Gatorade. A medical researcher at the University of Florida, he attempted to find a drink which would replace not only the water but also the salt and minerals in an athlete's body. The final mixture combined water, sodium, potassium, phosphate, and sucrose and glucose. During initial tastings, however, problems were uncovered, not least the large number of tasters who threw up violently while attempting to swallow the liquid. Bravely, Cade had a go and confirmed that, as feared, it tasted of piss. Fortunately his wife, a keen student of the film *Mary Poppins*, was on hand to suggest adding a twist of lemon and a spoonful of sugar. Bingo.

The product was used by the University of Florida's football team (The Gators) with immediate and remarkable efforts. While other teams wilted, they just kept on going. Cade had managed to bottle Duracell. The product is sold in 80 countries and in 2005 accounted for 80% of the $5.5 billion sports market. It is also used to combat diarrhoea.

# Homework

Mark the following examples of homework and see if you can do better . . .

Sven has a separate room in his house for his collection of 150 suits! What other sportspeople do you suspect need an extra room at their gaff and what would it contain?

- Rafa Benitez has a separate room as a nightclub so he can stand on the door like a bouncer trying to look trendy with a goatee beard.

- Wayne Rooney to apply for planning permission to build an extension for a granny flat.

- Ruud Van Nistelrooy needs a room to store his hay.

DEFEND THE INDEFENSIBLE
Arsène Wenger will capture the spirit of the FA Cup if he fields a team of Arsenal tea ladies.

*or*

Just like Ashley Cole, vomiting is a vital part of my love-making too (to Jim Jeffries).

ARTWORK

**Maradona, Diego:** Hand of God, penis of a mouse.
Explain with a drawing in the style of this book's cover. (Your
illustrated answer should showcase your knowledge of both biology
and current cloning practices.)

# Stats

## SHOW US YOUR MEDALS – MOST SUCCESSFUL SPORTING FOOTBALL FAMILIES

**The Laudrups** (36 major football honours): Michael Laudrup – won 7 league titles (1 Juventus, 4 Barcelona, 1 Real Madrid, 1 Ajax), 4 domestic cups (3 Barcelona and 1 Ajax), 3 European trophies (1 with Juventus and 2 with Barcelona) and 5 trophies as manager of Brondby; Brian Laudrup – 6 league titles (2 with Brondby, 1 with AC Milan, 3 with Rangers), 1 European Championship with Denmark, 2 domestic cups with Rangers, and 1 UEFA Super Cup; Finn Laudrup – father of Brian and Michael, former Denmark national football player; Ebbe Skovdahl Hansen – uncle of Brian and Michael and brother-in-law of Finn, successful football manager who has won four domestic league titles in Denmark and 3 domestic cup trophies all with Brondby; Mads Laudrup – son of Michael, plays as a central midfielder for Copenhagen; Andreas Laudrup – son of Michael, plays for Real Madrid Juvenil B.

**The Nevilles** (26 major football honours): Gary Neville – 13 trophies with Man Utd (8 League titles, 1 Champions League, 1 Intercontinental Cup, 3 FA Cups, 1 League Cup); Phil Neville – 11 trophies with Man Utd (6 League titles, 1 Champions League, 1 Intercontinental Cup, 3 FA Cups); Tracey Neville – sister of Gary and Phil, netballer, won Commonwealth bronze medal; Neville Neville – father, played cricket for Green Mount Cricket Club in Lancashire during the 1980s.

**The Charltons** (10 major football honours): Bobby Charlton – 1 World Cup, 3 League titles, 1 FA Cup, 1 European Cup; Jack Charlton

– 1 World Cup; Jack Milburn – uncle of Bobby and Jack Charlton, played for Leeds United. His cousin is Jackie Milburn who was a striker for Newcastle United and three-time winner of the FA Cup, and his brothers George, Jimmy and Stan Milburn all played professionally.

.......................................................................................................................................................................

**The Ferdinands** (6 major honours): Rio Ferdinand – winner of 3 League titles, 1 Champions League and 1 League Cup; Anton Ferdinand – brother of Rio, currently playing as central defender for Sunderland; Les Ferdinand – cousin of Rio and Anton, won the League Cup with Spurs in 1999 and is the 5th highest Premier League goal scorer.

**McARTHUR, ELLEN:** As Stuart Hall so eloquently described her achievement: 'She went seventy-eight days without SEX! What a woman. She must have a prosthetic in the cabin or an instrument on the poopdeck to keep her company.'

**MACHIAVELLI:** 'Christ! He could think.' Alex Ferguson.

**MaCLEOD, ALLY:** Perhaps the most grandiose national manager these isles have produced. Only Ally would have organised an open-top bus tour lap of honour round a packed Hampden Park before the tournament began. Only Ally would have spoken about not simply winning but retaining the World Cup before the tournament began. In the event, Scotland lost to Peru and drew with Iran. The 1973 Ayr Citizen of the Year winner bought a pub.

**McMAHON, STEVE:** His favourite male TV star is Lenny Henry, his favourite female star is Margaret Thatcher. If not a footballer he'd be a psychiatrist.

**MAGNIFICENT EXCHANGE RATE:** 'I've never once criticised South Africa. I love the country. The people are fantastic. The exchange rate is magnificent. The only thing I can't stand is the system in place in sport. It shut doors for me.' Kevin Pietersen.

**MAGNIFYING THE MIDGETS:** 'I don't care a brass farthing about the improvement of the game in France, Belgium, Austria or Germany. The FIFA does not appeal to me. An organisation where such football associations as those of Uruguay and Paraguay, Brazil and Egypt, Bohemia and Pan Russia, are co-equal with England, Scotland, Wales and Ireland seems to me to be a case of magnifying the midgets.' FA member Charles Sutcliffe (1928).

**MAKING IT MORE REAL:** Mark Lawrenson on the murder of Colombian defender Andres Escobar during the 1994 World Cup: 'The only way I can make it more real for people . . . it's like Tony Adams going away to the European Championship, scoring an own goal, coming home . . . and getting shot.'

**MANDELA, NELSON:** 'I hope you were as delighted as I was last weekend when Nelson Mandela was freed from a South African jail. But what I hadn't bargained for was the fact that his release was going to cut across the start of our Littlewoods Cup semi-final against Coventry.' Brian Clough.

**MARCA:** The Spanish newspaper summed up David Beckham's first season at Real Madrid as follows: 'His regression in the last few weeks is self-evident. First of all, he played and ran. Then he ran and played. Then he just ran. Now he neither runs nor plays . . .'

**MARINELLO, PETER:** The sixth Beatle. Subject of a most unseasonably violent debate during the first Christmas Special of *Fighting Talk*, when Jimmy Hill threatened to chin Dickie Davies for suggesting that Beckham was the best-looking footballer of all time. Hill's point was that Beckham had access to a far wider range of grooming and manicure products and therefore the playing field was not level.

**MEDICAL OLYMPICS:** 'Sports is not our forte. If there was a gold medal at the Olympics for doctors, engineers, scientists, we'd [India] pick up every time. Our country is based on education and the middle-class education is very high. Sport is by the way.' Kapil Dev.

**MEN'S VOGUE:** 'Any man who loves clothes should buy this magazine,' says Cardiff City's Jay Bothroyd. The word he uses most often is 'innit'.

**MEREDITH, BILLY:** Nicknamed Old Skin because of his long wiry frame, Meredith would chew on a toothpick as he danced and dribbled down the wing. An expert penalty taker, in the days when goalkeepers were not prohibited from charging forward from their lines, he would lob the ball over them and into the net. He played 48 times for Wales and in his last game, in 1920, beat England on their own ground. His final game was an FA Cup semi-final at the age of 49. On retiring he became a publican.

**MIDDLESBROUGH:** 'To be honest, racism never crossed me until I played for Leicestershire against Yorkshire at Middlesbrough and the crowd were throwing bananas at me and chanting certain things. I remember I was crying. Winston Benjamin, who was our overseas player, saw what was going on and swapped with me. He picked up one of the bananas, peeled it, ate it, threw it back into the crowd, smiled, and said "Thanks." I thought spot on. That is what my attitude should be.' Phil De Freitas.

**MIDGET BOWLING:** Banned by state legislators in New York in 1990. Much to the dismay of 3ft Australian, Mike Anderson ('My pals and I like it') and promoter Bryce Jones ('The sport is a performance art designed to satirise the values of mainstream America and not revolting like, say, naked females wrestling in jelly').

**MIND THE WINDOWS, TINO:** Freddie Flintoff standing at slip, while a twitchy Tino Best was flashing wildly at Lord's, said, 'Mind the windows, Tino.' Next ball Best, trying to hit the ball over the pavilion, was bowled all ends up.

**MONEY, MONEY, MONEY:** A leader in *The Times* (the paper of record) really did suggest that the following should be a World Cup song:

> Money, Money, Money,
> Get drunk, eat curry,
> In a rich man's world,
> Money, Money, Money,
> Make films like Vinnie,
> Stay in a rich man's world,
> Aha-ahaaa,
> All the blondes I can do,
> Now I've got a little money,
> I'm in a rich man's world.

**MONEY, SERIOUS:** 'Playing pool without serious money on the line is like Rudolf Valentino being chased by 400 gorgeous tomatoes, running into his hotel room and bolting the door and reading *Playboy* magazine.' Minnesota Fats.

**MOORE-BRABAZON, JTC:** A champion sledder, he was also the first man to attempt to refute the assertion that pigs couldn't fly. A rebuttal he carried off in some style at Leysdown in Kent in 1909 by strapping a pig in a wicker basket, with a sign reading 'I am the first pig to fly', to the wing strut of his aeroplane. Later, as the first Lord Brabazon of Tara, he would serve in Churchill's 1940 government as Minister of Transport before the public expression of his wish that the Germans and the Russians would exterminate each other necessitated a move sideways.

**MUTU, ADRIAN:** An exception to the rule that if you are shopping an adulterous footballer to the tabloids it is customary to be generous to a fault about their love-making. 'Transylvanian temptress Laura Andresan, 23', being less than complimentary as she bucked the trend in lurid, and damningly lucid, detail. It all started positively enough with a cut finger leading to some blood-sucking and, inexorably, a top of the kitchen table coupling. But things became murkier when they retired upstairs to join 'mutual friends' Crang and Anca (a cracking name for a pub) in the Bucharest flat's only bedroom. For a while each couple did their own thing but then Mutu 'must have realised he wasn't turning me on' (a horrible 'must' for Mutu; perhaps it dawned upon him when Laura told him, as she told the *Sun*, that 'he was like a beginner at sex – like a young boy with very little experience'). Whatever, Mutu switched to Anca. Sadly, for the long-term future of the foursome 'ex-Penthouse model Laura . . . didn't fancy Crang' (Crang's views are not recorded). Mutu returned to Laura but 'for all his money, good looks and charm, the great Mutu was not so great in bed. And when it was over I realised I didn't even like him very much.' Better late than never.

# Q&A

**NAME:** Greg Brady

*Greg sits at* Fighting Talk's *top table. He has been on the show since the beginning and is a contender for the winningest* Fighting Talk*er ever. Currently co-hosting the Bill Watters show on Toronto radio station CFMJ, Greg also provides co-commentary for BBC 5 live's Superbowl coverage. He follows the fortunes of Chelsea, the Miami Dolphins and the Detroit Red Wings ice hockey team and Detroit Tigers baseball side.*

**FAVOURITE *FIGHTING TALK* QUESTION?:** Do you have cricket fever?

**FAVOURITE *FIGHTING TALK* ANSWER?:** Absolutely not. Physically impossible.

**WHICH WORD OR PHRASE IS MOST OVERUSED ON *FIGHTING TALK*?:** Golden envelope. It just sounds dirty.

**WHICH FOOTBALL TEAM DO YOU SUPPORT?:** Chelsea and Man City – with the exchange rate, I get two.

**WHICH SPORTING PERSON DO YOU MOST IDENTIFY WITH?:**
Dennis Wise. I play hockey that way. Annoying.

**FAVOURITE PERSON IN SPORT?:** John McEnroe.

**LEAST FAVOURITE PERSON IN SPORT?:** Alex Ferguson.

**MOST EMBARRASSING SPORTING MOMENT?:** Losing a tennis match at age 20 to a 36-year-old who was smoking in between games.

**WHAT IS YOUR LEAST FAVOURITE SPORTING GIFT RECEIVED?:**
My *Fighting Talk* mug.

**GIVE ME YOUR BEST SPORTING STATISTIC:** A Canadian team hasn't won the Stanley Cup in 16 seasons.

**STRANGEST INJURY SUFFERED ON A SPORTS FIELD?:** Ripped shorts . . . on the butt . . . while playing football. Finished the match. I'm a gamer.

**WORSE SPORTING BET YOU HAVE MADE TO DATE?:** Holland to win Euro 2000 – I put a LOT of coin on them and to watch them lose after Italy had two men sent off . . . disastrous.

**WHICH IS THE MOST BEAUTIFUL KIT IN SPORT?:** Man City's sky blue. It just is. Sweden's hockey jerseys are great, too.

**WHAT IS YOUR SPORTING WEAPON OF CHOICE?:** Left-handed hockey stick.

# The *Fighting Talk* Award for Cricket's Biggest Niggler

And the nominations are:

1. **WG GRACE:** Who kidnapped Billy Midwinter from Lord's in 1878 when he was padded up to open the Australian innings against Middlesex and re-sourced him south of the river to play for Gloucestershire at the Oval. He would go out for the toss with a coin featuring Queen Victoria on one side and Britannia on the other, toss it, and shout not heads or tails but 'Woman!'

2. **DOUGLAS JARDINE:** 'The Iron Duke' was stunned when, before the first Test of the Bodyline Tour, Australian journalists approached him and asked for the names of the English team. 'Let me make it perfectly clear once and for all,' said Jardine, 'that I never speak to Australians.' Matters only got worse for the Australians.

3. **ARJUNA RANATUNGA:** Set something of a record when breaching five of the nine stipulations in the ICC Code of Conduct during a single one day international, managing to comprehensively rile the Australians, who weren't even playing. Shane Warne says: 'Without doubt the most difficult cricketer I've met or played against is Sri Lanka's captain, Arjuna Ranatunga.'

The big man's skill was to turn his inherent laziness into an effective art form. One of his best ploys was his use of runners. When not employing a runner he was the pre-eminent walker of a single of this or any other generation. 'I like people talking about my weight and I like walking my singles in Test cricket. I wouldn't recommend it to young players but I reckon I've won more overthrows in the past 10 years than any player in the world.'

Best of all, Captain Cool as he is known in his homeland, speaks his own language. 'He always has plenty to say,' says Warne, 'although he usually speaks in his own language to annoy us even more and avoid getting into trouble with umpires.' Not only is he a talented linguist but he is also a gifted ventriloquist. 'He has the ability to talk without his lips moving so no one can pick up on it,' says Michael Slater.

Before the World Cup final Steve Waugh said, 'Those fucking Sri Lankans are going to fucking get what's fucking coming to 'em.' Captain Cool responded by putting the Aussies in and, a few hours later, scoring the winning run.

And the joint winners, for niggling Australians so effectively and so effortlessly: Jardine and Ranatunga.

# Homework

Mark the following examples of homework and see if you can do better . . .

It didn't take much imagination for the producers to come up with the dismal TV format – *Wags Running a Boutique!* So we want you to be a bit more creative at home and come up with suggestions for other shops for sports people.

- Greg Brady could open an English language college for American kids . . . with the first lesson: 'Right lads, who can pronounce the forward known as Yakubu?'

- Colin Montgomerie should open a specialist bra emporium.

- Audley Harrison should open a massage parlour; with those big hands and his ability to go down quickly he would finally have a big hit.

- Alan Curbishley could open a jumble sale buying rubbish, selling rubbish and talking rubbish.

DEFEND THE INDEFENSIBLE
For me this has been the best *Fighting Talk* ever, two gay men in the studio (to Greg Brady, Canadian and father of two).

*or*

Darfur? Schm-arfur.

MULTIPLE CHOICE

The phrase 'handbags' has multiple meanings. When you hear it do you immediately think of:

1. An off-the-ball stabbing conducted by two or more overpaid tarts.

2. A money-wasting competition between permatanned partners of national heroes.

3. Sol's got more of them than Freddie.

By all means give more than one answer.

## WORST LOSING STREAKS IN SPORT

- California Institute of Technology College Basketball Team: Had an 11-year, 207-game NCAA Division III losing streak dating back to 1996.

- Luxembourg National Football Team: Lost 26 international games in a row between 2003 and 2006.

- Tampa Bay Buccaneers: NFL team lost all their games in the 1976 season which was 14 games, the only team to experience a winless regular season.

- Cleveland Spiders: MLB team who recorded a 24-game losing streak in 1899, which is supposedly the longest MLB losing streak in history. The Philadelphia Phillies came closest to breaking this record with a 23-game losing streak in 1961.

- Cleveland Cavaliers: The team with the longest losing streak in the NBA; in the 1981–82 season they lost their last 19 games of the season, which when combined with the five losses at the start of the 1982–83 season, constitute the NBA's all-time longest losing streak of 24 games.

- Sunderland FC: From 18 January 2003 to 10 September 2005, lost 20 games in a row in the Premier League (if you don't include the break for being in the Championship after being relegated in 2003, or any FA Cup results in 2003), probably the longest losing streak in the Premiership.

**NADAL, RAFAEL:** 'Has the biggest onions in sport,' Brad Gilbert.

**NEDVED, PAVEL:** Speaking out on behalf of footballers against war. 'We sportsmen didn't want this war. Whether it's right or wrong I cannot say. Above all we need to think of the children.'

Maybe 100 years: 'I'd like to say my name is Benjamin Sinclair Johnson Jnr and this world record will last 50 years, maybe 100.' So said Ben Johnson after trimming four-hundredths of a second off the world record to finish first in the 100m at the Seoul Olympics in 1988.

**NEWMARKET:** 'Not so much a one horse town as an all horse town.' Jonathan Meades.

**NORMAN, ANDY:** Husband of Fatima Whitbread. Aged 23 he became the youngest ever sergeant in the Met. He gave up being a copper, however, in order to look after athletes including Steve Ovett, Brendan Foster and Sebastian Coe. Pretty soon he was effectively every athlete's agent and said to be paid £30,000 a year by Nike. 'No one was breaking the law,' he said about his agenting, 'just the rules of the sport.'

**NORMAN, MORGAN AND ASTON:** Only Greg Norman would name both his children after the cars in his garage.

**NUDD MBE, BOB:** The brains behind fishing's first rap record – 'Maggots in Ya Catapult'. Subject of a mass vote from the fishing community for Sports Personality of the Year but the BBC rigged the vote, even though, this being pre phone-in days, there wasn't a penny in it for them. Pure spite.

**NUTRITION IS THE QUEEN:** 'When I started using weights, sixty years ago, they all said I was a nut. Now people who don't use weights will be left behind in the lurch. The next big change will be food, diet. Here's a good slogan: Exercise is the King, Nutrition is the Queen, and together they formulate a great kingdom and its universe is productivity.' Gary Player.

**NUTTER:** 'I signed [Marco] Boogers off a video. He was a good player but a nutter. They didn't show that on the video.' Harry Redknapp.

# Q&A

**NAME:** Simon Day

*Stand-up comedian, actor and Competitive Dad among other characters from* The Fast Show, *Simon has established himself as a* Fighting Talk *favourite. He has a huge passion for boxing and describes himself as an England football fan. He is known on the show for brilliant answers but often falls at the final hurdle with his defend the indefensible.*

**WHAT ARE THE SKILLS NEEDED FOR *FIGHTING TALK*?:** Not talking over the travel news is one.

**FAVOURITE *FIGHTING TALK* OPPONENT?:** My own diction.

**FAVOURITE SOUND EFFECT?:** They are all a blur to me.

**MOMENT WHEN YOU THOUGHT *FT* WAS MOST LIKELY TO BE TAKEN OFF AIR?:** There would be an enormous uprising of fat bald men, it wouldn't happen.

**WHICH WORD OR PHRASE IS MOST OVERUSED ON *FIGHTING TALK*?:** Err . . .

**ANY OTHER BUSINESS:** I need to sell my car.

**WHICH FOOTBALL TEAM DO YOU SUPPORT?:** England.

**WHICH SPORTING PERSON DO YOU MOST IDENTIFY WITH?:**
Eric Bristow.

**FAVOURITE PERSON IN SPORT?:** Jimmy White.

**LEAST FAVOURITE PERSON IN SPORT?:** Mark Viduka.

**PROUDEST PERSONAL SPORTING MOMENT?:** Winning the cup
and championship at cricket for my primary school. I scored the
winning runs.

**MOST EMBARRASSING SPORTING MOMENT?:** I have let a lot of
terrible goals in at a lot of different levels.

**FIRST SPORTING MEMORY?:** England losing to Germany in 1970.

**WHICH SPORTING SKILL WOULD YOU MOST LIKE TO HAVE?:**
World-class playmaker who could tackle and play the piano really
well.

**WHAT IS YOUR MOST TREASURED SPORTING POSSESSION?:**
My boxing books.

**WHAT IS YOUR LEAST FAVOURITE SPORTING GIFT RECEIVED?:**
A ticket to see Millwall *v* Chelsea at Chelsea, kicked unconscious!

**GIVE ME YOUR BEST SPORTING STATISTIC:** Ninety-nine per cent
of English footballers can't retain possession.

**WORSE SPORTING BET YOU HAVE MADE TO DATE?:** John Virgo
to win the Embassy snooker every year for eight years.

**WHAT'S BEEN THE STRANGEST SPORTING EVENT YOU'VE EVER SEEN?:** Bare-knuckle fighting in Lee Green or cock fighting in Thailand.

**WHAT'S BEEN THE BEST SPORTS EVENT YOU HAVE WITNESSED?:** Joe Calzaghe *v* Jeff Lacey.

**WHAT IS YOUR SPORTING WEAPON OF CHOICE?:** Kung fu stars.

# The *Fighting Talk* Award for Greatest Dive in a Competitive Football Match

**ROBERTO ROJAS:** Chile were struggling during a World Cup qualifier against Brazil in 1989. Plan A had failed, Plan B wasn't working, so Rojas skipped through the alphabet to Plan Z. To wit, force an abandonment and a replay in a neutral venue. On 69 minutes, therefore, he subtly threw himself into the smoke of a firecracker, which had landed nearby, pulled a razor blade from his glove, and stabbed himself in the head. The plan could not have worked better. There was blood everywhere, a mass brawl, a walkout, and an abandonment . . .

If only CCTV had never been invented. Video evidence revealed the extent of Rojas's scheming. Brazil were awarded the game, Chile were kicked out of the 1990 World Cup and excluded from the next, Rojas was banned for life and the woman who threw the firecracker was signed up by *Playboy Brazil*. In May 2001, Fifa lifted the ban. 'At 43, I'm unlikely to play again,' said Rojas, now coach at São Paulo, 'but at least this pardon will cleanse my soul.'

# Homework

Mark the following examples of homework and see if you can do better . . .

*The Simpsons* celebrates 20 years this week . . . we are nothing if not predictable but if we don't do it now we'll never do it . . . can I have your sportspeople as Simpsons characters . . .

- Gary & Phil Neville could be Patty & Selma coz they're both overshadowed by their better-looking sister and have bouts of dodgy facial hair.

- Smithers would be Colin Montgomerie's caddy, as they both work closely with Monty and like to get their hands on his shaft and give tips on his grip.

- Sven-Göran Eriksson could be Mayor Quimby. Clueless about his job, dodgy back-handers and ropey women.

- Mourinho would be Sideshow Bob. Clearly more intelligent than some of the clowns he has to work with, but you can't help feeling that he would try kill you if you stood in his way.

DEFEND THE INDEFENSIBLE
The haka is like Riverdance – but gayer.

*or*

Joe Calzaghe should be stripped of his titles purely because he is Welsh (to John Rawling, ITV boxing commentator).

**Sepp Blatter:** The one-time Head of Public Relations of the Valaisan Tourist Board in Switzerland is, among other things, a winner of the prestigious International Humanitarian of the Year award. He divides the nation. Is he also . . .

A bespectacled buffoon and administrator who brought the game into disrepute with his daft ideas?

*or*

A clear-headed and far-sighted visionary whose thoughts on women footballer's shorts were ten years ahead of their time?

# Stats

## FOOTBALL'S GREATEST JOURNEYMAN

- **JOHN BURRIDGE:** Goalkeeper John Burridge is often
  regarded as the quintessential journeyman footballer. And
  with very good reason! He made league appearances for 15
  English league clubs and five Scottish league clubs in a
  27-year career. He was also on the books of four English
  league clubs and one Scottish League club without playing
  games for them, and also had spells at six non-league clubs –
  a grand total of 31 clubs.

  Football League Clubs (15): Workington, Blackpool, Aston
  Villa, Southend United, Crystal Palace, Queen's Park Rangers,
  Wolverhampton Wanderers, Derby County, Sheffield United,
  Southampton, Newcastle United, Scarborough, Lincoln City,
  Manchester City and Darlington.

- **LUTZ PFANNENSTIEL:** If Burridge is famous for being a
  home-grown journeyman (one without a passport if you will)
  then Pfannenstiel is football's greatest global journeyman. He
  is mostly famous for having played for 20 different clubs all
  around the world during his career, including stints in New
  Zealand, Singapore, Finland, Malaysia, Canada and Albania.
  He is currently playing in Flekkerøy IL in Norway and is the
  only player to have played professional football for clubs in
  all six continents.

  Football Clubs: FC Bad Kötzting, Penang FA, Wimbledon,
  Nottingham Forest, Sint-Truidense, Hamrun Spartans,
  Sembawang Rangers, Orlando Pirates, Nottingham Forest,
  TPV, Nottingham Forest, SV Wacker Burghausen, Geylang

United, Dunedin Technical, Bradford Park Avenue, ASV Cham, Dunedin Technical, Bradford Park Avenue, Dunedin Technical, Bærum SK, Calgary Mustangs, Otago United, KS Vllaznia Shkodër, Bærum SK, Vancouver Whitecaps, Clube Atlético Hermann Aichinger and Flekkerøy IL.

- **RUDI GUTENDORF:** German football manager, renowned for managing the highest number of national teams – to date a total of 17 teams.

  International Teams managed:

  1.  Chile (1972–73)
  2.  Bolivia (1974)
  3.  Venezuela (1974)
  4.  Trinidad & Tobago (1976)
  5.  Grenada (1976)
  6.  Antigua & Barbuda (1976)
  7.  Botswana (1976)
  8.  Australia (1979)
  9.  New Caledonia (1981)
  10. Nepal (1981)
  11. Tonga (1981)
  12. Tanzania (1981)
  13. Ghana (1985), Nepal (1986)
  14. Fiji (1987)
  15. Zimbabwe (1995)
  16. Mauritius (1997)
  17. Rwanda (1999).

# O

**ODESSA, TEXAS:** A town ranked:

1. Fifth worst in America (*Money* magazine).

2. Seventh most stressful city in America – based on alcoholism, crime, divorce, suicide et al (*Psychology Today*).

3. 'Worst town on earth' (Larry McMurtry in *Texasville*).

And yet Permian High School, Odessa, Texas has four times come out as the best team in Texas and, by Texan extension, the best team in the world.

They spend more per annum on medical supplies for the football team than they do on teaching materials for their entire English department.

**OFFICERS:** 'I want the lads. If it is confined to officers, I'm not bloody playing.' Michael Caine in *Escape to Victory.*

£80,000 a week: 'For Sol Campbell to be on £80,000 a week at Arsenal is ridiculous. I think Campbell represents the market's peak.' One-time Barings employee Nick Leeson.

**OLIO, NANCY DELL:** 'Yes, I care about fashion, but today I want to talk about peace. I was talking to Sven and I said, "Privileged people like us, celebrities, we have to do something." So I had an idea that maybe we could use the power of football for good. I thought, let's build a football pitch in a war-infected area.'

**OLIVER, TED:** Charismatic journalist who had his nose bitten by Vinnie Jones. As the blood poured Jones said, 'I always do that to people.' Oliver responded by calling for a photographer not a doctor. Jones was small beer. When Oliver met the Loyalist paramilitary 'Mad Dog' Adair, his opening question was, 'Do I call you Mr Mad or just Dog?'

**ONE OF THE WORST I'VE SEEN:** 'In 2002 he was outflanked, in 2004 he was outwitted. The substitution of Rooney for Vassell was one of the worst I've seen in international football.' Alan Hansen on Sven-Göran Eriksson.

**OSAMA BIN LADEN:** 'I will fight to clear my name. I've been made more hated than Osama Bin Laden.' Jonathan Barnett, Ashley Cole's agent.

**O'SULLIVAN, PETER:** When awarding Piggott with a Special Award for Services to Racing during the 1995 programme, Peter O'Sullivan said, 'Lester, I have to admit, that annually for 41 years I have expected your unique talent to be recognised by BBC TV Sport. I'm rather sad that it's so belated but I'm very proud and very honoured to present you with this unique trophy which is in recognition of your utterly unique talent.'

**OWN PLANES:** 'One or two of the guys have their own planes,' says American Ryder Cup golfer Scott Verplank, 'and they have said as soon as we start bombing Iraq, they will be on the way.'

# Q&A

**NAME:** Gary O'Reilly

*Gary is a former central defender for Tottenham Hotspur, Brighton & Hove Albion, Crystal Palace and Grays Athletic. He famously opened the scoring in the 1990 FA Cup final against Manchester United and has made a successful career as a sports broadcaster since retiring from the game.*

**PROUDEST *FIGHTING TALK* MOMENT?:** First win, you always remember your first win, unless you're an ex-pro who headed footballs for a living and even trained to head footballs then it's all a big blur, bit like The Stones and the 60s or was it the 70s.

**WHAT ARE THE SKILLS NEEDED FOR *FIGHTING TALK*?:** Loads of bullshit, good memory (see above answer for reason why lack of wins), depth of knowledge and full Internet access to Wikipedia.

**WHICH FOOTBALL TEAM DO YOU SUPPORT?:** Spurs, since age of six

**FAVOURITE PERSON IN SPORT?:** Hmm . . . Well I like them as athletes, but generally not so sure that I like them as people.

**PROUDEST PERSONAL SPORTING MOMENT?:** Making debut at 19 for club supported as a boy and coming on as sub and kicking Mike Channon up in the air immediately. Shows you dreams do come true.

**GIVE ME YOUR BEST SPORTING STATISTIC:** I am 6'1" not the 5'11" the Rothmans book always said I was. Think I'm the only defender to score in both semi- and final of the FA Cup in the same year.

**WHICH IS THE MOST BEAUTIFUL KIT IN SPORT?:** Tottenham early 70s, Real Madrid all white pre-sponsorship, original Ajax from early 70s and Brazil 1970.

**WHAT'S BEEN THE BEST SPORTS EVENT YOU HAVE WITNESSED?:** FA Cup final Sunderland v Leeds United.

**WHAT IS YOUR SPORTING WEAPON OF CHOICE?:** Javelin, I was former county champion. Start running.

**TELL US ABOUT YOUR STRANGEST SPORTING DREAM:** Mid-December 1980. Dreamt I was playing for Spurs first team and was elbowed in the face running towards my own goal by a striker. December 27th made full debut at Carrow Road v Norwich. Chasing ball back to own goal Justin Fashanu elbowed me in the face, just as I had dreamt.

# The *Fighting Talk* Award for Most Combative Chairman

And the nominations are:

**JESUS GIL:** Disappointed to be convicted for fraud, Jesus reacted by offering to kill his Atlético players ('I mean it, some of the players don't deserve to live'), withdraw their salaries ('and anyone who doesn't like it can die'), and gave the year's best radio interview, days after having a pacemaker fitted. 'There's too many bloody passengers in this team! They're not going to laugh at this shirt any longer! They are not going to make fun of me . . . Carreras, Santi and Otero are no good. They can die!' (Interviewer tries to cool things, reminding Gil about his new pacemaker.) 'I'm sick of people telling me to relax! They can stick my heart up their arses!' He went on to deny blowing $800,000 of Atlético Madrid's money on women's underwear ('No one told me there was a prohibition on panties and bras.').

*and*

**KEN BATES:** A chairman of the Old School. He was uninterested in placating fans with big money purchases and more taken with exploring the possibilities of having them caged in behind crocodile-infested moats. In the 1970s an Irish Court stated that the one-time dairy farmer was not a suitable man to run a company. He went on to run Oldham, Chelsea and Leeds.

If reincarnated, which seems a long shot, frankly, he would like to come back as a general or a bishop. Or, possibly, both.

And, with Ken Bates being deducted a regulation fifteen points, the winner of the trophy is Jesus Gil.

# Homework

Mark the following examples of homework and see if you can do better . . .

Mrs Chris Coleman was so worried she bugged her husband's car. Whose car would you like to put a listening device in and what would you expect to hear?

- I'd bug Lance Armstrong's car to see if he too says 'BLOODY CYCLISTS. Why don't they look where they are going?'

- I would bug Alan Shearer's car. He HAS to say something interesting at some stage – I think it's important for mankind that it is documented.

- Although not strictly a sporting answer, I'd like to put a bug in Steve Bunce's car – just to see how many times the young lady replies – 'Would you like fries with that?'

DEFEND THE INDEFENSIBLE
Premiership footballers should be forced to wear veils.

*or*

It's the corporate guests that really bring the atmosphere to an FA Cup final.

QUESTION
**Golfers Choking:** Are you a Norman man or a Sanders man when it comes to golf's biggest choker?

**Norman:** In the opening round of the 1996 Masters Greg Norman shot a course-record 63. Three days later he contrived to go round the same 18 holes at Augusta National in 15 strokes more. In so doing he blew a six-shot lead – the biggest in Masters history – over Nick Faldo and converted it into a five-shot deficit. For ever more known as the Great White Flag.

**Sanders:** Having two putts from 30ft to win the 1970 Open at St Andrews, he left his first putt 30in short. 'I was confident standing over it, and then I saw what I thought was a little piece of sand on my line,' says Sanders. 'Without moving my feet, I bent down to pick it up, but it was a piece of grass. I didn't take time to move away and get reorganised. I mishit the ball and pushed it to the right of the hole. It was the most expensive missed putt in the history of the game.'

# Stats

**SLIGHTLY MORE THAN A BAKER'S DOZEN OF FOOTBALLERS WHO MIGHT UNDERSTAND THE STATS IN THIS BOOK**

- **Sócrates:** Graduated as Doctor of Medicine from Faculdade de Medicina de Riberirão Preto, the medical school of the University of São Paulo, whilst playing professional football for Botafogo. Also holds a doctorate degree in Philosophy and is currently a practitioner of sports medicine in his home town.

- **Iain Dowie:** Has a master's degree in Engineering (M.Eng) from University of Hertfordshire and became employee of British Aerospace whilst playing non-league football for Cheshunt.

- **Norman Whiteside:** Studied originally at the University of Salford. Upon retirement from football he studied to become a podiatrist and now works for the PFA.

- **Steve Palmer:** Former QPR player, studied at Cambridge University before playing football. According to rumour, he achieved a First in maths, and rumour is good enough for us (see Steve Bunce).

- **Espen Baardsen:** Completed Open University degree having retired from football at 25 and is now a financial analyst for London-based hedge fund Eclectica.

- **Shaka Hislop:** Graduated with honours with a degree in Mechanical Engineering from Howard University in USA and also interned at NASA.

- **Arjan de Zeeuw:** Has a degree in Medical Science and plans to go into sports medicine after football.

- **Stuart Ripley:** Graduated in 2007 from University of Central Lancashire with first-class honours in Law and French, going on to UCLan's Lancashire Law School and a post-graduate Legal Practice course

- **Slavan Bilic:** Graduate of Law faculty in Split. Speaks fluent German, English and Italian (plus Croatian presumably), and plays in rock band called Rawbau.

- **Steve Coppell:** completed degree in Economic History at Liverpool University whilst at Man Utd.

- **Gavin Peacock:** is currently doing a Theology degree at Cambridge in between appearances on *Fighting Talk*.

- **David Wetherall:** Former Leeds footballer, gained first-class honours in Chemistry at the University of Sheffield in 1992 apparently . . . (see Steve Bunce).

- **Steve Heighway:** Former Liverpool footballer, part of the successful team of the 1970s, graduated from the University of Warwick with a degree in Economics whilst playing non-league football.

- **Graeme Le Saux:** Went to Kingston University before he played football, doesn't say what degree he achieved but nevertheless clearly the most qualified man ever to appear on *Fighting Talk* (bar Gavin Peacock).

# P

**PARK, REG:** The British Arnold Schwarzenegger. Two feet wide at the shoulders with a 32in waist and biceps measuring 18 1/2in, he was twice Mr Universe and, according to Arnie, the first of the peplum (sword-and-sandals) film heroes. He would drink a gallon of milk a day and eat a dozen eggs.

**PATTERSON, FLOYD:** The first heavyweight to retain the World title (against Ingemar Johansson in 1960). Born in Waco and trained by Cus D'Amato. He was dismissive of amateurs: 'I say this now without shame. Line up a dozen amateurs and guarantee me $250,000 for fighting each one and I'll take them on one after another.'

**PECK, M SCOTT:** *Golf and the Spirit – Lessons for the Journey.* Most usefully Scott Peck has created his own imaginary golf course (called the Exotica Golf and Tennis Club) and dedicated a chapter to each hole. Thus we have Hole 5 Human Nature, and Hole 15 Golf and Sexuality, and Hole 18 God. Scott Peck says, 'Upon occasion I have vaguely wished that I could write something that was not about God, but I cannot . . . Certainly you do not have to believe in God to play golf – even great golf. Nonetheless, I suspect it helps.'

**PEE WEE REESE:** 'Pee Wee Reese was a shortstop from Louisville Kentucky and freely admitted that he had very mixed feelings about having Jackie [Robinson] on the team – he was a creature of his time,' remembers team-mate Lester 'Red' Rodney. 'Yet it was he [Reese] who said, in a Kentucky drawl you could have laid, "Democracy means everyone should be treated the same, yet Jackie is the only coloured guy in the League and he's getting special hell for it. Maybe we ought to do something to make it more equal." In Cincinatti once there was a group of men shouting vile things at Jackie and no one was stopping them. And Pee Wee dropped his glove, walked across the diamond, and draped his arm around Jackie Robinson. That was a tremendous big deal at the time.'

**PENNE ARRABIATA:** Ex-England and Charlton fullback Chris Powell's favourite meal.

**PEOPLE, CUNNING:** 'Football is made for cunning people. It was always like that and it will always be like that. I'm not thinking about being a role model for my sons or for the fans watching me. I don't think it is true to say that you are disloyal to football if you feign an injury, or tug a shirt or do something else to win the game as winning games is the purpose of football. Cheating the referee is not a sin if it helps your team to win. I was born a defender and I'll die a defender.' AC Milan's Pablo Montero.

**PEP, WILLIE:** Arguably, the greatest defensive boxer of all time, he once won a round without having thrown a punch. Nicknamed Will o' the Wisp he said, 'They call Ray Robinson the best fighter pound for pound. I'm the best fighter, ounce for ounce.' His first big fight came when someone tried to take over his shoe-shine pitch. 'We fought like pigs for 20 minutes. The blood was spurting out of my nose and my stomach felt like it was coming apart, but somehow or other, I hung on. After that, nobody ever bothered me again.' His 229 wins constitute a record that is most unlikely ever to be broken.

**PESCHISOLIDO, PAUL:** The most famous person he has met is not, perhaps surprisingly, wife Karen Brady but Michael Jackson. He explains, 'It's a tough one, but it would have to be Michael Jackson. When I was at Fulham, Mohammed al Fayed invited him to the club and he came into the dressing room one day to meet us before a game. It was a very bizarre experience, he was trying to talk to us about football but he did not have a clue! It was brilliant.'

**PETTYS:** The First Family of NASCAR are the Pettys from Level Cross, Randleman, North Carolina. The only four-generation family of athletes in major league American sports. There's grandaddy Lee, who was in at the beginning, racing alongside Junior Johnson, dubbed 'The Last American Hero' by Tom Wolfe, and the Flock brothers – Bob, Tom and Fonty. There's Daddy Richard who is the acknowledged 'King' of the sport and known as Elvis. There's pony-tailed Kyle who runs Petty Enterprises now. And his little boy Adam who is just starting out. In true *Little House on the Prairie* style, Kyle compares running the family NASCAR team to having kids: 'When Adam was born, everybody in the world wanted to babysit him. You could set him out in our front yard, set a sign beside him and people would stop by and want to babysit him. Then Austin came along and they didn't come no more, it was only family would babysit. Then you get three and you don't have no family any more.'

**9/11:** *'This is all wonderful news. The US and Israel have been slaughtering the Palestinians, just slaughtering them, for years. Robbing them and slaughtering them. Nobody gave a shit. Now it's coming back to the US. Fuck the US. I want to see the US wiped out. Death to the US.' Bobby Fischer on Filipino Radio.*

**PHASE OF PLATEAU:** Gerard Houllier: 'You call our season a step back. I call it a phase of plateau.'

**PIETERSEN, KEVIN:** According to a textbook tabloid sting, KP is 'a nervous lover' who preferred to go about his work in silence although he was partial to having his full name shouted repeatedly towards the end of proceedings. That's KEVIN PETER PIETERSEN.

**PING-PONG:**

1. 'Regard a ping-pong ball as the head of your 'capitalist enemy. Hit it with your socialist bat and you have won a point for the fatherland.' Chairman Mao.

2. This is my seventieth year of ping-pong playing,' Henry Miller wrote in 1971. 'I started at the age of ten on the dining room table. The focal point in my house is the ping-pong room. I take on players from all over the world. I play a steady, defensive Zen-like game. The importance of my recreation lies in preventing intellectual discussions. No matter how important or glamorous an opponent may be, I never let him or her distract me.'

    And they were often distracting. Miller played ping-pong at Clichy with Anaïs Nin, with Chaim Soutine at the Villa Seurat, with Lawrence Durrell in Corfu, at a Paris bistro with Brassaï, in Hollywood with Man Ray . . .

**PINOCHET, GENERAL AUGUSTO:** While 'staying' at Wentworth seriously considered setting up a consortium with former PM Margaret Thatcher and former song'n'dance man Tommy Steele to buy Reading. However *Auto Trader* magnate John Madejski saw them coming.

**PLAIN STRAIGHT BALL:** Having heard Fred Trueman bang on about his inswinging yorker, his slower ball and his late outswinger, an exasperated team-mate asked Fred if he had ever bowled a plain straight ball. 'Aye, I did,' replied Trueman, 'and it went straight through like a stream of piss and flattened all three.'

**PLAYER, GARY:** Also known as 'The World's Most Travelled Athlete' and 'The Black Knight' and 'Mr Fitness' and 'The Man in Black' and 'The International Ambassador of Golf'.

**Majors:** 9
**Air Miles Travelled:** 21,874,823 (as of 01/06/08)

**PLAYGROUNDS, SCHOOL:** 'You can go to any school playground and learn all you want to know about oral and anal sex from a ten year old.' Thank you, Stuart Hall.

**POLONIUM:** 'Yeltsin, Gagarin, Lenin, Polonium, Ivan The Terrible, Tolstoy, Gorbachev, Ra-ra-Rasputin, Sharapova, Tchaikovsky, Abramovich . . . Israel will give you boys a hell of a beating.' *Sun* front page. And 'the Middle East minnows' did their job, only for Croatia to beat England.

**PRETTY BORING:** 'Like I say, I think the Tour, the ATP Tour, is pretty boring. There's nothing to do . . . I think press is pretty boring, that's why I don't laugh . . . I think being here and travelling all year, going from hotel to hotel, is not a life anyone wants to have.' Chilean tennis player Marcelo Ríos, the pony-tailed one-time Number One.

**PRIVACY:** 'I am a high-profile person and my privacy should be down to me, Andrew Cole, not to a taxi driver or anyone else who would wish to drive me around.' So said Andy Cole before going on to claim that he needed a car for 'his charity work' and was 'too famous' to use a bus.

**PUB LEVEL:** 'After the game Sepp Blatter escorted me from the referees' dressing-room to the DVD area, we sat in silence reviewing the evidence, and at around 11.30 pm we realised that, for me, following 23 years of hard work, working up from pub level, my dream was over.' Graham Poll.

**PUSKAS, FERENC:** Architect of Hungary's 6–3 victory at Wembley in 1953. He scored 83 goals in 84 appearances for Hungary, 357 times in 354 games for his club Kispest (renamed Honved) and 512 times in 528 games for Real Madrid. He supported the anti-Soviet uprising before escaping, with his family, to Vienna. At Real he scored four in the 7–3 European Cup final victory over Eintracht Frankfurt and a second-half hat-trick in the loss to Benfica 5–3. Quietly plump, he was nicknamed the Galloping Major. He said, 'The ball should be moved early, preferably on first contact. To run with it is often only to waste valuable attacking time.'

**PUTNEY TRAVELODGE:** The billet of choice for Jelena Dokic, who stayed there for the Wimbledon Championships which she entered as a qualifier before going on to knock out Martina Hingis in the first round and making it to the semi-finals. Despite her achievements a trend was not established.

# Q&A

**NAME:** Douglas Anderson

*Dougie 'two answers' Anderson, as he is affectionately known, brings a certain style to the* Fighting Talk *studio with his sharp dress sense. He is a television presenter with a number of different credits from RI:SE to* T in the Park *for the BBC. He follows the fortunes of Hibernian Football Club and can often be found with the tartan army following his beloved Scotland. In 2003 he was in the top five of Scotland's Most Eligible Men.*

**FAVOURITE *FIGHTING TALK* QUESTION?:** What is your favourite Fergie moment?

**FAVOURITE *FIGHTING TALK* ANSWER?:** My favourite Ferguson moment was before a Champions League match at Galatasaray, where journalists kept asking if he was worried about taking his stars into hell, to which he simply replied, 'You've obviously never been to a wedding in Clydebank.'

**BIGGEST *FIGHTING TALK* REGRET?:** Not going to the toilet before a particular show.

**WHAT IS YOUR MOST TREASURED SPORTING POSSESSION?:**
The programme for the first football match I ever went to. Hibernian
v Aberdeen, October 1983. At the time Aberdeen were the reigning
European Cup Winners' Cup champions and managed by Alex
Ferguson. Brilliantly Hibs won 2–1. It was also the day I heard some
rather juicy swearwords for the first time.

**WHAT IS YOUR LEAST FAVOURITE SPORTING GIFT RECEIVED?:**
I was once given swimming trunks. There are some items you
should always buy yourself such as contraception or dental
insurance. Trunks fall into this category. Thankfully they were
handed over without that most dreaded of sentences: 'We're about
the same size, I tried them on in the shop to check and they fitted
fine.'

**GIVE ME YOUR BEST SPORTING STATISTIC:** Gordon Smith is the
only player in the history of Scottish football to win the League title
with three different teams. What makes this all the more
remarkable is that he never played for either of the Old Firm!

**WHICH IS THE MOST BEAUTIFUL KIT IN SPORT?:** The classic
Juventus black and white stripe or the retro chic of St Etienne's
strip of the 70s.

# The *Fighting Talk* Award for Female Olympian

**ELEANOR HOLM:** Holm travelled to the 1936 Olympics as the reigning 100m backstroke champion having been unbeaten for seven years. During the voyage she fell into the company of sportswriters and collapsed after a night-long champagne 'n' dice session. The team physician diagnosed acute alcoholism. Holm argued in her defence that she was 'free, white and 22'. Avery Brundage, leader of the US delegation, expelled her. Two hundred US athletes, including Jesse Owens, signed a petition demanding her reinstatement. Brundage ignored it. Holm spent the Olympics socialising with Goebbels and Goering, the latter gave her a silver swastika from his uniform.

Uniquely for an Olympic athlete of the time, Holm spent her time in between swims dressed in a white bathing suit and stetson and singing 'I'm an Old Cowhand'. Having retired from swimming, she went on to appear in the film *Tarzan's Revenge*, in which she was knocked unconscious for an hour by an over-enthusiastic extra. This marked the beginning and end of her movie career.

She was spotted by Billy Rose, 'the little Napoleon of Showmanship', whose song credits included 'Does the Spearmint Lose its Flavour on the Bedpost Overnight?' and 'I Found a Million Dollar Baby (in a Five and Ten Cent Store)'. He cast her alongside Johnny Weissmuller and Buster Crabbe in the world's first

'Aquacade'. Holm performed with credit, although sustained exposure to chlorine turned her hair green.

At the time of their marriage Rose referred to his wife as 'Holm sweet Holm'. Their divorce, which followed on from an old flame of Rose's committing suicide in their Manhattan apartment, was labelled by the press as 'The War of the Roses.'

# Homework

Mark the following examples of homework and see if you can do better . . .

To celebrate Mother's Day, which sportsman would make the best mum?

- Wayne Rooney would be a great mum: imagine chips for breakfast, chips for dinner and chips for tea!

- Colin Montgomerie would make a great elderly mum: he has the breasts, he is a bit of an old woman and when he is not suffering from pre-menstrual tension he gets hot flushes.

- Thierry Henry would make a fine mum. He has to carry his team for at least nine months of the year.

- Arsène Wenger: a complete old woman and never sees her kids do anything wrong.

- Any of many Premiership footballers. No matter what, they'll always have a roast ready at the weekend.

DEFEND THE INDEFENSIBLE
I miss Steve Bunce's Rumour Mill even more than Princess Diana.

*or*

I won't be watching the Champions League final on Wednesday because Steve Bunce will be coming round and I have recorded 'Any Dream Will Do' (to John Rawling).

QUERY HEADING

If West Ham could field a team of eleven Billy Bondses, they would never be relegated. Discuss with reference to the following facts:

**England Apps:** 0
**Age on Last Appearance for the Club:** 41 years and 225 days
**Highest Basic Wage:** £600
**First Job on Being Appointed Coach:** Painting the dressing-room

# Stats

## LIFE EXPECTANCY OF TOP DIVISION WINNING MANAGERS SINCE 1950

| Manager | Age at Death |
| --- | --- |
| Arthur Rowe | 93 |
| Matt Busby | 84 |
| Tom Whittaker | 58 |
| Stan Cullis | 84 |
| Ted Drake | 82 |
| Harry Potts | 75 |
| Bill Nicholson | 85 |
| Alf Ramsey | 79 |
| Bill Shankly | 68 |
| Joe Mercer | 76 |
| Harry Catterick | 65 |
| Bertie Mee | 82 |
| Brian Clough | 69 |
| Don Revie | 61 |
| Bob Paisley | 77 |
| Joe Fagan | 80 |

# Age of Death of Top Division Winning Managers since 1950

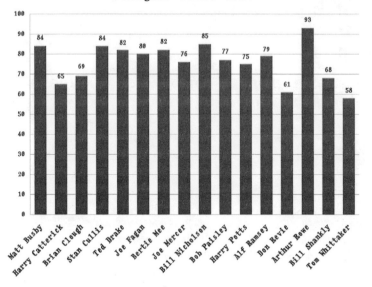

*Mean = 75.47*
Average life expectancy for UK males = 76.23
Top division winning managers life expectancy closest to = US Virgin Islands 75.4 years for males (26th highest life expectancy overall in the world)

## Q&A WITH PETER OSGOOD:

**Q:** Which pubs did you use around Stamford Bridge?
**A:** The Black Bull and Rising Sun were right by the ground and we would pop in those sometimes, but we used to go down the Kings Road most of the time for our serious drinking. We used to use pubs like The Trafalgar, The Chelsea Drugstore and the Markham Arms. Alexander's was our main restaurant, and we used to go to the Pheasant Tree, which was a great club restaurant. The Eight Bells was another pub we used, and it was a great place because we would sit at the table and there was a telephone there, so people used to phone us up and ask if they could come over for a drink, and we would say yes, or no. If they were pretty and female we tended to say yes. Those were our main hangouts really.

**Q:** What is your big passion outside of football?
**A:** Chardonnay!

*More Indian women watched the 2007 Brazilian Grand Prix than British men.*

## Q&A WITH A YOUNG LESTER PIGGOTT:

**Q:** 'What is your favourite racecourse?'

**A:** (long pause) Newbury.

**Q:** Is this because of the setting, the ground, the gentle roll of the course?

**A:** No, it's nearest home.

**QUEL IDIOT:** When Belgium keeper Filip De Wilde trod on the ball to let Sweden in for the opening goal in Euro 2000, RTBF's commentator lost it. 'What a cunt!' he screamed, before calming down and adding for emphasis, 'what a cunt!' RTBF later toned down the commentary for replays – replacing it with the rather anodyne 'Quel idiot! Quel idiot!'

**QUESTION:** Never more ridiculous than when fearless friend of the punter Channel 4's Derek Thompson, Tommo, is doing the asking. Example: the 2008 Cheltenham Gold Cup is over and jockey Ruby Walsh has quite evidently picked the worse of trainer Paul Nicholls' two horses:

**Tommo:** Any thoughts now about whether you should have gone for Denman or whatever?

**Ruby Walsh:** That's probably the most ridiculous question I have ever been asked.

**Tommo:** It is, I know, but I had to ask you.

**Walsh:** No, you didn't have to ask me.

**A QUESTION OF SPORT:** The stats are extraordinary. Born 5/1/70. Shows to date: 812. Hosts: Three (Vine, Coleman, Barker) Audience for 200th edition: 18 million. Record number of appearances: McCoist (363). Guests on first show: Lillian Board, Tom Finney, George Best and Ray Illingworth.

# Q&A

**NAME:** Ian Stone

*A successful stand-up comic and a regular guest on* Fighting Talk.
*He was born in London into a Jewish family and is a huge Arsenal
fan. During his extensive* Fighting Talk *career he has made finishing
third into an art form.*

**FAVOURITE *FIGHTING TALK* QUESTION?:** We were once asked to
describe how we looked and I said that I moved with the grace of
Thierry Henry. Radio's great.

**FAVOURITE *FIGHTING TALK* ANSWER?:** I was moaning about
Steve McClaren and I said that he's always looking for the positives
in any situation and that if his entire family was wiped out by a
terrible house fire, he'd be stood at the door going 'obviously that
wasn't the result we were looking for but we have to look for the
positives'.

**WHICH SPORTING PERSON DO YOU MOST IDENTIFY WITH?:**
Arsène Wenger. A grievous sense of injustice and a love of the
beautiful game.

**PROUDEST PERSONAL SPORTING MOMENT?:** Scoring a header

from a corner in Battersea Park and learning to swim when I was thirty-four.

**WHAT IS YOUR LEAST FAVOURITE SPORTING GIFT RECEIVED?:** My friend Yvonne once gave my one-year-old son a Newcastle shirt. She's not my friend any more.

**STRANGEST INJURY SUFFERED ON A SPORTS FIELD?:** Having my nose broken going for a diving header in a Maccabi League division two game. Anyone who knows me knows that this is not an insubstantial thing.

**WHAT'S BEEN THE STRANGEST SPORTING EVENT YOU'VE EVER SEEN?:** I went to a baseball game in Tokyo and it seemed like a game from another planet.

**TELL US ABOUT YOUR STRANGEST SPORTING DREAM:** I've scored numerous winning goals for Arsenal over the years. I remember scoring the winner in a 4–3 game against Spurs and I took off my shirt and had the most amazing flat stomach. Even in the dream, I knew that this couldn't be.

# The *Fighting Talk* Award for Best Table Top Game - Subbuteo

Invented by Peter Adolph it was intended to be called 'The Hobby' but for patent reasons had to be named after the Latin name for the hobby bird, *Falco subbuteo*. At its peak in the early 8os there were, conservatively, nearly seven million players. It was the game of the green baize and the little plastic men, marketed under the slogan 'flick to kick'. The 'must-play' game for the discerning adolescent with few friends.

Accessories included a VIP Presentation Set complete with plastic mini-Queen, 'material for keeping the ball in the net' and a choice of miniature Ken Baileys. (See Paedophile memorabilia)

Jonathan Pearce, the suicidally enthusiastic 5 live commentator, played an entire World Cup Competition, including *all* qualifying groups plus the playing of appropriate National Anthem before each game.

No other children's game (not Cluedo, not Kerplunk, not Escape from Colditz) was mentioned in songs by not one but two of the hipper bands of the early 8os, both of whom would regularly make it into John Peel's Festive Fifty. First: The Undertones 'My Perfect Cousin' featuring an irritating relative who can flick to kick and by

God he knows it. Second: Half Man Half Biscuit's 'All I Want for Christmas is a Dukla Prague Away Kit' which ended with the haunting refrain:

'And your travelling army of synthetic supporters,
Would be taken away from you and thrown in the bin.'

Far from being a sign of a wasted youth (excepting, obviously, Snooker Express), playing Subbuteo proved, for many, to be an aid in later life. Not least because mastering a game involving a multitude of ambidextrous flicks stood them in good stead when, at some time in the distant future, it was incumbent upon them to handle a clitoris.

# Homework

Mark the following examples of homework and see if you can do better . . .

England rugby skipper, Phil Vickery, has the words 'I'll fight you to the death' tattooed on his arm. How about some words that other sportspeople might like inked on their bodies?

- Sven could have a handle tattooed on his feet so that when he is so far up David Beckham's arse you could see something to pull him out with.

- Audley Harrison has a tattoo on his jaw saying 'Fragile – Handle with Care'.

- Dotted line on Cristiano Ronaldo's ankle with the words "TRIP HERE".

DEFEND THE INDEFENSIBLE
The government should buy Jens Lehmann for the nation.

*or*

Let's get off OJ's case – he's a single father for goodness' sake.

ESSAY
**Chapman, Lee:** On the field – plodding journeyman. Off the field – over-vigorous love-maker. Discuss this contradiction with references to other seemingly contradictory sportsmen (Gascoigne, Boycott, and the rest).

# Stats

## BRITAIN'S OLDEST LIVING SPORTSPERSON

- A BBC Special on 11 February 2005 reported on a team called Egor RFC, a club recognised by the RFU that caters for players over the age of 40. At the time the BBC reported on a player named Des Pastore, who was 90 at the time and considered the oldest active sports player in Britain. Assuming, and it's a routine assumption, he is still playing, he would be 93. The second oldest player at the time was Billy Gregory, who was 80. The players wear coloured shorts according to their age so opposition players know how hard to tackle them – "When you're 50 you get black, 60 is red and 70 gold. When you turn 80 you get purple shorts and, if you're still playing at 90, you can wear whatever colour you like, it's a miracle you're there and we're just glad to see you,' says the octogenarian Billy Gregory.

- *The Northern Echo* reports an active bowls player on 14 February 2008 whom they claim to be the oldest active sportsman in Britain at the age of 98, called Bob Murton. Bob was busy playing and declined to comment.

- Jack Hyams was the oldest cricketer to play at Lord's at the age of 81 having played for Cross Arrows in 2001. He is still active, with a team called Nomads reporting that he is their oldest active player at the age of 87.

- Ivor Powell, the former Welsh footballer, at 91 is the oldest active football coach in the world, currently as manager of Team Bath.

**RADCLIFFE, PAULA:** Some unchivalrous panellists have claimed that she makes them come over all gay . . . but not Stanley Vernon Collymore. On the first ever show the banter was temporarily interrupted for an update on the Paris Marathon from Pat Murphy (or Matt Purphy as Christian O'Connell repeatedly called him to his great irritation). While Purphy reported on Paula's progress, Stanley turned round to the rest of the panel and asked, 'You would, wouldn't you?' 'Would what?' one of the more naive panellists replied. 'Give her one,' said Collymore and then moving his forearm horizontally backwards and forwards provided a somewhat graphic description of how he would carry out the task.

**RAMIFICATIONS:** 'It would be irresponsible not to say that this defeat will have ramifications, especially for Steve McClaren.' John Motson at the conclusion of England 2, Croatia 3.

**REACHING ADOLESCENCE:** 'My life revolved around the ball. But as I reached adolescence I started getting attracted to the opposite sex. I got a girlfriend and although I wanted to become a professional player, it wasn't my highest priority.' José Mourinho.

**RED BULL OR TWO:** 'On game day I get myself ready and then have a Red Bull or two and then I'm sorted.' Kevin Pietersen.

**REED, AUSTIN:** When Tony Jacklin became Ryder Cup captain he demanded the three Cs: Concorde. Caddies. Cashmere. He also refused to wear 'awful clothes with braiding everywhere'. Instead, he wanted his team decked out in 'Austin Reed, a very reputable name.'

Twice as many people of Lebanese descent live in Brazil (7 million) as in Lebanon.

**RELIGIOUS FERVOUR:** 'Over the last decade a religious fervour seems to have hit American golfers, and they cannot win a tournament without thanking the Almighty. If there is a God, I just could not see him taking a beer out of the fridge, putting his feet up and taking a serious interest in the outcome of a golf tournament; surely he would have more important things to do. I may be cynical in this respect (maybe God is a huge golf fan), but the way some of their players feel God is very much on their side, maybe they should be handicapped a couple of shots for having an extra caddie or calling on an outside agency.' Mark James.

**RIBENA:** 'I love the original blackcurrant one,' admits Notts Forest's Kris Commons. 'The other's OK, but blackcurrant's still the first and best.' If he were not a footballer Kris would probably be doing something with Motocross. He would like to meet Ben Stiller but 'not at dinner or anything like that in case it got a bit awkward.'

Southampton's Jason Euell says, 'You can't beat Ribena.'

**RIIHILAHTI, AKI:** For a while the undisputed champion of the worldwide websites. Sample contribution following the theft of his mobile: ('RETURN MY NOKIA YOU BASTARDS'): 'Easter was crucial not only to my mobile but also to Palace's season. Our Via de la Rosa, the route of destiny, ended with results that stopped our play-off hopes. That hurts. We got some nice football but the reality is one point and arrivederci Eagles. The common rule is don't try to exert yourself when you already have shit in your pants.'

**RON, BIG:** A manager renowned for bringing a bit of glamour to half-time talks as Dean Saunders recalls: 'So it's half time at the Villa and we were having a bit of a disaster, Big Ron would follow the players on with his boiling head on and say, "Sit down everybody." The door would open and in comes Rene, one half of the famous Rene and Renata and Ron says to the lads, "Sit down and just have a look at what passion really means!" Rene would then stand there singing Nessun Dorma with his face turning purple, and while this is going on I'm trying to tell Ray Houghton which runs I'm planning for the second half and Ron looks at me with an icy stare and puts his finger to his lips. And then at the end of the song he says, "That is what passion is about. Now get out there and show those supporters what you are made of!"
And this wasn't just a one-off. He tried Robbie Williams singing, Stan Boardman telling jokes . . . no wonder he never won anything at the Villa.'

**ROOSE, DR LEIGH RICHMOND (1883–1917):** Known as the 'Mad Doctor' he played in goal for Everton, Sunderland and Arsenal and won 24 caps for Wales. An eccentric amateur, he once completed a match without having to remove his overcoat. In another, after the Welsh full-back was injured, he doubled up as goalkeeper and overlapping full-back. Wales won 8–0.

**ROUGH, ALAN:** The only goalkeeper at the 1978 World Cup not to wear gloves. Scotland failed to qualify from their group.

**ROVER, THE NEW:** Proved to be a deal breaker in Eddie McCreadie's negotiations with Chelsea after he had won them promotion. 'It was Eddie's fault, really. They offered him the new Rover, which was Car of the Year, and he held out for a Mercedes.' Peter Osgood.

**RUDDOCK, RAZOR:** Once claimed that Lord Brocket is 'the funniest man I've ever met in my life.'

Club Apps: 358 Goals: 30
England Apps: 1 Goals: 0
Weight Before Entering Jungle: 19 stone 2 lbs
Weight On Leaving Jungle: 13 stone 11 lbs
(NB This leaves Razor second in the all time lists for greatest weight loss registered during a celebrity TV programme. Celebrity Fat Club's Andy Fordham is top with a breath-taking loss of 7 stone 1 lb)

**RUDE AND INSINCERE PEOPLE:** Chelsea's Steve Wicks has always disliked them.

**RUSH, IAN:** Really did say 'I couldn't settle in Italy – it was like living in a foreign country'. During a less than successful stay at Juventus was often photographed reading the *Gazzetta dello Sport* upside down.

Club Apps: 602 Goals: 254
Wales Apps: 78 Goals: 28
Manager: Chester City
Number of Italian Words Mastered during Time at Juventus: 4

**RYDER CUP, 1991:** When the event was contested in the aftermath of Desert Storm, some of the American players confused their vowels and seemed uncertain whether they were competing in a Golf War or a Gulf War. One of their most confused players was a camouflaged-capped Corey Pavin.

**RYDER CUP, 2006:** A quarter of the European team was Irish, a quarter of the American team didn't have passports before the match.

# Q & A

**NAME:** Iyare Igiehon

*Iyare began presenting the breakfast show for 1Xtra in 2002 when the station launched He currently presents the show* In The Mix *on BBC 6 Music and works across BBC Radio 2 and also BBC 1Xtra. Iyare is a passionate Arsenal fan and grew up a stone's throw from the ground in Finsbury Park.*

**BIGGEST LIE TOLD ON *FIGHTING TALK*?:** The suggestion that I was ever any good at sport.

**GIVE ME YOUR BEST SPORTING STATISTIC:** 10 keepie uppies . . . in a row!

# The *Fighting Talk* Award for Defensive Play - Alex Erlich

The 1936 world Table Tennis Championships in Prague proved to be something of a watershed for table tennis. This is because Poland's Alex Ehrlich turned up with one deeply held ambition – to prove to the world that he was the greatest chiseller the sport had ever seen. To chisel in table tennis is to refuse to attack under any circumstances and simply to bide your time in defensive play until your opponent falters. In Italian football terms, it is *cattenacio* with knobs on.

His first round match was against Farcas. The first point of their match lasted 2 hours and twelve minutes as Ehrlich using his special, outsized 'chiselling bat' to great effect. After seventy minutes the score was still 0–0, but Farcas, accoding to a witness, 'had shrivelled with every return and now looked like a hunchbacked robot.' Nor was Ehrlich looking entirely comfortable. 'The extra weight of his chiselling bat had begun to tire his arm, so he 'deftly switched his bat and contunued the point left-handed.' And the umpire wasn't looking too clever when after 85 minutes of head-turning arbitration his neck locked in one position. A replacement was summoned. Meanwhile the ball having crossed the net more than twelve thousand times, and with Farcas' arm beginning to freeze, the first point was decided in Ehrlich's favour.

Twenty minutes into the second point, a member of Ehrlich's team reached into this equipment bag and pulled out a knife, a long loaf of bread and a two foot polish sausage. This was too much for Farcas, who had not come prepared for a winter siege. Provoked beyond reason, he started to attack and then, in a fit, 'sent the ball and bat together sailing wildly over the King's head' and 'ran screaming from the court.'

Embarrassed by Ehrlich's antics, the ITTF decided to 'invigorate' the sport of ping-pong. It decreed that a game had to stop after twenty minutes, the victory going to whoever was ahead. Ehrlich would later spend four years at Auschwitz and was only saved from the gas chamber because the Nazis recognised him as the World Champion.

# Homework

Mark the following examples of homework and see if you can do better . . .

Could you give me a few lines of an obituary for a currently living sportsperson . . .

- Here lies Emile Heskey. Sadly missed . . . again.

- An obituary for Arsène Whinger . . . He was hit by a truck which, unfortunately and with cruel irony, he didn't see.

- Alex Ferguson: Born Scottish, lived angry, died red.

- Jonny Wilkinson: I *told* you I was ill.

### DEFEND THE INDEFENSIBLE
To reflect the ethnic diversity of this country Gordon Brown should insist that 25% of all players representing England are Polish.

*or*

I strongly advise anyone who's running the London Marathon to pocket the sponsorship money.

### ESSAY
'Arsène Wenger is the most overrated manager in England.' Despite having the largest football video library in the world in his faux Georgian mansion on the outskirts of Romford (see *Guinness Book of Records 2007* – 35,000 videos of football matches from around the globe, all arranged alphabetically), his record as Arsenal manager has been patchy. George Graham won 2 titles in 9 years,

and crucially a European Cup Winners' Cup final against a team containing Gianfranco Zola. Wenger, in contrast, has won only three titles in a dozen years, despite having markedly better players, and has won less in Europe than Dana International.

# Stats

**WHICH EUROPEAN LEAGUE IS THE MOST VALUABLE OUT OF FORBES TOP 20 MOST VALUABLE FOOTBALL TEAMS FOR 2008?**

| Team | Value ($m) | Value (£m) | Country |
| --- | --- | --- | --- |
| Man Utd | 1800 | 911.31 | England |
| Arsenal | 1200 | 607.54 | England |
| Liverpool | 1050 | 531.60 | England |
| Chelsea | 764 | 386.80 | England |
| Tottenham Hotspur | 414 | 209.60 | England |
| Newcastle Utd | 300 | 151.88 | England |
| Olympique Lyonnais | 408 | 206.56 | France |
| Bayern Munich | 917 | 464.26 | Germany |
| Schalke | 470 | 237.95 | Germany |
| Borrusia Dortmund | 323 | 163.53 | Germany |
| Hamburg SV | 293 | 148.34 | Germany |
| Werder Bremen | 262 | 132.65 | Germany |
| AC Milan | 798 | 404.01 | Italy |
| Juventus | 510 | 258.20 | Italy |
| AS Roma | 434 | 219.73 | Italy |
| Inter Milan | 403 | 204.03 | Italy |
| Celtic | 227 | 114.93 | Scotland |
| Real Madrid | 1285 | 650.57 | Spain |
| Barcelona | 784 | 396.93 | Spain |
| Valencia | 254 | 128.60 | Spain |

Premiership teams clearly dominate the top 20 list and make up just over 42% of the total value, followed by Spain, Germany and then Italy.

## Percentage of Total Value of Top 20 Most Valuable Football Teams

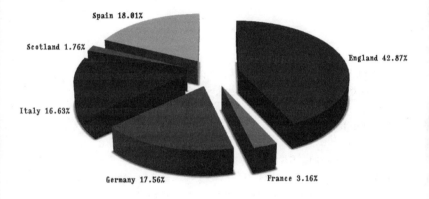

Spain 18.01%

Scotland 1.76%

England 42.87%

Italy 16.63%

Germany 17.56%

France 3.16%

# S

**SAMBURU TRIBESMAN:** Intriguingly, a member of this Kenyan tribe appeared in an Adidas commercial seemingly mouthing 'Just do it'. In fact he was saying, 'I don't want these. Give me big shoes.'

**SANYO HI-FI, SANYO VIDEO AND, MOST POETICALLY, SANYO HI-FI NEEDLE TECHNOLOGY:** Three of the biggest names in show-jumping in the 70s.

**SATURDAY, A:** Arnie Palmer's favourite sandwich is peanut butter and jelly. Known as a 'Saturday', one side is refrigerated and the side with peanut butter toasted. The toasted bread is usually wheat bread while the refrigerated piece of bread is typically potato bread.

**SAVAGE, ROBBIE:**
**Club Apps:** 420 **Goals:** 30
**Wales Apps:** 39 **Goals:** 2
**IQ:** 167 (Coincidentally the same number as Robbie's highest televised darts finish)
**Total transfer cost:** £6,150,000

Tennis: 30–40 is the most vital point and deuce or 30–30 the second most important. The advantage that is gained from serving first in a set could be immediately removed if, as in the tie-break, player A serves the first game and then player B the second and third and so on.

**SCHINDLER'S LIST:** Fulham's Antti Niemi's favourite film. 'I know it's not the happiest film ever made, but I thought it was a great story,' he explains.

**SCHOOLS, PUBLIC:** The rules and ethos of the working man's game were devised and developed in these 'timelessly elitist' establishments. Cheltenham College invented the throw-in, Harrow the concept of sending off a player who wilfully broke the rules and Eton contributed the offside principle with its rule against 'sneaking'.

**SCHROEDER, TED:** The only commercial refrigeration equipment seller to have won the gentlemen's singles at Wimbledon (1949). Having done so he was on the point of turning professional but instead became Vice President of the Kold Hold Pacific Sales Company.

**SERIE A:** Perhaps the best letter ever published in the half-decent football magazine *When Saturday Comes* went as follows: 'Whatever the rights and wrongs of the Iraq conflict, I was deeply concerned by reports that the Americans plan to move on next to Serie A. What have the Italians done to deserve that? And whatever next? The Nationwide Conference?'

**SERIOUS HORSES:** 'There are some serious horses in Ballydoyle, all you can do is hope you get the job done right. It's up to me to make the most of the ammunition.' Kieron Fallon.

**SEWELL, EHD:** In his no-nonsense *Rugger: The Man's Game*, Sewell proposed a post-war Ministry of Sport and Compulsory Rugger.' This idea has yet to take hold, although Alistair Campbell did set up focus groups after England won the World Cup to see if 'Rugger could be made to work for Labour'.

**SEX:** Dr Jukn Sztajzel from the University Hospital of Geneva has done some helpful research into sex and athletic performance. He has found that sex two hours before an event increases heartbeat and lowers endurance. But any sex enjoyed ten hours before has no effect.

**SHADOWS ON THE GRASS:** 'The filthiest book ever written about cricket.' EW Swanton. Written by Simon Arthur Noel Raven, described by EW as having 'the mind of a cad and the pen of an angel'.

**SHAG, GREAT:** The girl allegedly roasted simultaneously by three Man United stars at their Christmas party ('Blame it on the Rio') according to *The Sun* 'bragged' about it afterwards to a 'sickened' party guest. The guest said: 'The men were shrieking like hyenas – it was vile. I asked the girl if she was OK and she said "Yeah, of course, why wouldn't I be? They said I was a great shag!" Then she hobbled off down the corridor.'

**SHARAPOVA, MARIA:** 'The kind of 16-year-old who'll get in a car and feel completely comfortable giving you directions,' says Tracy Austin. 'She's a hard worker with amazing discipline who makes decisions promptly.'

   **Career Prize Money:** $12,030,153
   **Career Record:** 300 – 68
   **Career Titles:** 19
   **Highest Ranked:** 1
   **Length of Right Leg:** 3 feet 4 inches
   **Length of Left Leg:** 3 feet 3 inches (she wears sponsored 'uplifts' in her left gym shoe)

**SIGN IN THE LOBBY OUTSIDE KEN BATES'S OFFICE:** 'The Romans did not build an empire by organising meetings. They did it by killing anyone who got in their way.'

Squash: When offered the chance of playing to nine or ten you should opt for the latter unless 'you assess your current chance of winning a point as under 38%.'

**SIMON PURES:** 'As sports fans, we prefer to dream about angels on wheels, Simon Pures somehow immune to the uppers and downers of our own pill-popping society. There is, all the same, a certain nobility in those who have gone down into God knows what hell in search of the best of themselves. We might feel tempted to tell them they should not have done it, but we can remain secretly proud of what they have done. Their wan, haggard looks are for us an offering.' Antoine Blondin on the Tour de France.

**SKIMMED MILK:** Fulham's Antti Niemi's favourite drink. He says 'I really enjoy drinking skimmed milk.'

**SMERTIN, ALEXANDYIV:** Once transferred for two wagonloads of coal.

**SMOKED MUTTON:** Alfe Inge Haaland has a passion for smoked mutton.

**SMOKING:** In 1998, FOREST, the pro-smoking lobby, selected the following tobacco-fuelled football team: Dino Zoff; Sócrates, Gerson, Jack Charlton, Frank Leboeuf, Jimmy Greaves, David Ginola, Osvaldo Ardiles, Malcolm Macdonald, Bobby Charlton, Robert Prosinečki. Sub: Gazza. Coach: César Luis Menotti.

**SOCIETY LIVING:** 'There needs to be discipline. It depends what society we want to live in. If we want to go over red lights then there will be accidents and some will be fatal and others not fatal.' David Dein on Ashley Cole.

**SOUTH OF FRANCE:** 'Much too good for the French,' says Reading's John Curtis.

**SPECIAL STUFF: ENGLAND v BRAZIL 1970:** 'A match for adults,' said Brazil manager Zagalo. After watching the film of it Bobby Charlton said, 'Even we were impressed. You could take that film and use it for coaching. That is what the game at the top is all about. There was everything in that, all the skills and techniques, all the tactical control, the lot. There was some special stuff played out there.'

**SPENCER, JOHN:** First Crucible winner of the World Championship and the first man to make a tournament 147 (The Holsten Lager Invitational in 1979). Irritatingly, the cameramen were on a tea break so no footage remains.

Figures: 'I can make figures say what I want.' Barry Hearn.

**SPONTANEOUS APPLAUSE:** 'I played a little bit of extra time, waiting until play was at the Kop end, before sounding the final shrill blast . . . the fans behind the goal burst into spontaneous applause. It was longer and louder than normal, even for a big home win. Did they know it was my final visit? Was it applause for me? They are such knowledgeable football people, it would not surprise me.' Jeff Winter in *Who's the B*****d in the Black? Confessions of a Premiership Referee.*

**SPORTS:** 'In the 60s music was the mode, the most important means of communication; that's where the highest values of the race were being articulated. I don't think that's the case today. I think today it's sports – that's where our most intense imagination is invited to manifest itself. The sports figures in America are much more attractive, much more interesting and their lives are much more dangerous than the rock figures. They are in the traditional heroic mode.' Leonard Cohen

**SPORTSWRITERS, RELATIVELY ELITE:** 'I remember being shocked by the sloth and moral degeneracy of the Nixon press corps during the 1972 presidential campaign – but they were like a pack of wolverines on speed compared to the relatively elite sportswriters who showed up in Houston to cover the Super Bowl.' Hunter S Thompson.

**STELLING, JEFF:** 'It's down to the final minute of the final game. Absolutely astonishing stuff. Derby 0, Coventry 0; Dunfermline 1, Celtic 2. And I hope this is accurate news for Carlisle fans' sake . . . [takes a breath] . . . Carlisle have scored in the last minute of their game against Plymouth. Unconfirmed. We hear that Jimmy Glass, the goalkeeper, has scored for Carlisle. He was taken on loan after Carlisle had sold their only goalkeeper on deadline day and the League gave them special dispensation to sign Jimmy Glass. Now if this is the case, and we're waiting for confirmation, it would be the most staggering story of the day.' Sky Soccer, May 1999.

**STEVE:** 'I want to look at players like Steve Guppy and Steve Froggatt,' Kevin Keegan, while England manager.

**STICKY DAY:** 'We're just really chuffed with the performances we're getting from the players. A couple of them are wide London boys and they are enjoying themselves. The real test for us will be when that sticky day comes.' Alan Pardew.

**STRAW, JACK:** Once really did write about diving footballers: 'And I just offer this thought – If there is no action, those in charge might reflect that the next time their wife, or mother or son or daughter is the victim of yobbish behaviour in the street, the perpetrator might have thought it was OK to show no respect because their heroes act in the same way on a Saturday.'

No 5: The position in the charts reached by Peter Osgood singing a cover version of Middle of the Road's 'Chirpy Chirpy Cheep Cheep'.

**STUDIO 54:** 'I was blown away. I went up to the gallery once with a friend of mine. You gotta be kidding me, what things were going on. Porn movies were like tiddlywinks compared to the stuff going on. Men and women. Women and women. Men and men. The weird thing is sometimes we used to bring our wives. They would say, "Why did you bring us?" I don't know.' Giorgio Chinaglia, ex-Swansea centre forward who scored 242 goals in 254 games in America.

**STUDYING GERMAN:** 'One of my sons is studying German – in case they try another invasion. You can never tell with the Germans.' Brian Clough.

# The *Fighting Talk* Award for Most Assiduous Sporting Parent

**EARL WOODS:** Born the son of a Baptist and epileptic street cleaner, his father, Miles, was renowned for being able to swear for thirty minutes without interruption. Earl was the first black baseball player in the Midwestern college leagues and had to eat and sleep on his own on road trips. He named Tiger, the son from his second marriage to Tida, after a South Vietnamese officer, Colonel Phong, who saved his life. By the age of three his son was shooting 48 on the back nine at the Navy Course in Cypress, Orange County. At four he was receiving professional instruction and listening to motivational tapes. They seem to have worked. His father's predictions, however, became ever more grandiose. Before his son had so much as won a Masters he was saying, 'Tiger will do more than any other man in history to change the course of humanity . . . He's the bridge between the East and the West . . . he is the Chosen One. He'll have the power to impact nations. Not people. Nations. The world is just getting a taste of his power.'

The marriage unravelled. Earl couldn't stand Tida's Thai cooking, and she couldn't stand his smoking. Ever more conscious that he might be the father of the Son of God, Earl Woods made appropriate arrangements, turning the house where Tiger had grown up into a shrine. 'I have prepared this house,' he said, 'so that it can be converted into a national historical monument one day. All the floors in here are granite; they are not hardwood or any of that other stuff. Granite – the hardest stone. All of the wood you see is walnut. It is built to last – because I am certain that one day the birthplace of Tiger Woods is going to become widely acknowledged.'

# Homework

Mark the following examples of homework and see if you can do better . . .

Bolton's top place in the Premiership was described in the *Telegraph* as 'like finding a piece of glass in a cream cake', so get your poetic hats on this week and give me your best sporting similes.

- Football managers are like wine. You want to buy English but just can't.

- Winning the Scottish Premiership is like being Liz Taylor's seventh husband. You know how to do it but how on earth do you make it exciting?

- The FA are like a fart in a crowded lift – someone's responsible but nobody will admit to it.

- Steve McClaren is like a new Barbie doll with pre-installed voice recordings, good at giving meaningless advice sound bites and afraid of getting wet.

DEFEND THE INDEFENSIBLE
Monk throwing should be an Olympic sport at the Beijing Olympics in 2008.

*or*

The Irish should be banned from the Cheltenham Festival.

## QUESTION

Give marks out of ten for the following Gingers, place them in a formation of your choice, and write an appreciation (not more than 50 words) of your Ginger of the Match.

- Paul Scholes
- Ray Parlour
- Neil Lennon
- Stuart McCall
- Gordon Strachan
- Alexi Lalas
- John Arne Riise
- Alex McCleish
- Billy Bremner
- Nicky Butt
- Alan Ball

If you have time feel free to speculate on how your team might fare against the Blondes, the Brunettes, the Beards etc, etc.

# (OUR ANSWERS) SHOW US YOUR MEDALS GINGERS!

**Paul Scholes:** 15 (8 Premierships, 3 FA Cups, League Cup, 2 Champions Leagues, Intercontinental Cup)

**Ray Parlour:** 9 (3 Premierships, 4 FA Cups, League Cup, European Cup Winners' Cup)

**Neil Lennon:** 13 (2 League Cups, 5 Scottish Premierships, 4 Scottish FA Cups, 2 Scottish League Cups)

**Stuart McCall:** 12 (Division Three, 6 Scottish Premierships, 3 Scottish FA Cups, 2 Scottish League Cups)

**Gordon Strachan:** 10 (2 Scottish Premierships, 3 Scottish FA Cups, Cup Winners' Cup, Super Cup, FA Cup, 1st Division, 2nd Division)

**Alexi Lalas:** 0

**John Arne Riise:** 7 (French League, French Super Cup, FA Cup, League Cup, Champions League, 2 European Super Cups)

**Alex McCleish:** 12 (3 Scottish Premierships, 5 Scottish Cups, 2 Scottish League Cups, European Cup Winners' Cup, Super Cup)

**Billy Bremner:** 7 (2 1st Division, 2 Fairs Cups, FA Cup, League Cup, 2nd Division)

**Nicky Butt:** 11 (6 Premierships, 3 FA Cups, Champions League, Intercontinental Cup)

**Alan Ball:** 2 (World Cup, 1st Division)

# T

**TABLE FOOTBALL:** Invented in 1924, the sport enjoyed its heyday in the 70s when the Mafia took an interest after noticing that the tables could usefully double up as drugs containers.

**TABLE TENNIS:** 'A shy sport played by shy people.' Howard Jacobson.

**TAEKO:** A young Japanese woman told the *Shukan Post* about her favourite man: 'I stayed at hotels where Beckham stayed during the World Cup. I checked toilets he might have used, took photographs of them and licked them. I'm definitely going to England. I want to live in Beckham's neighbourhood and go swimming or shopping with him. If I meet his wife Victoria, I will ask her to leave him.'

**TAKING UP THE MANTELPIECE:** Rio Ferdinand talking about captain Gary Neville being injured: 'Giggsy has stepped in and taken up the mantelpiece.'

**TENNIS:** 'Really brings out the best in women, I find.' Peter Osgood.

**TEXTBOOK ILLUSTRATION:** 'Football is a textbook illustration of the internal contradictions of globalisation in the period of the nation state,' says Professor Eric Hobsbawm.

**THEAGENES:** Noted Roman athlete. He was so successful that a fellow competitor used to sneak into the Temple and mutter threats and imprecations against his rival's idol. One day, perhaps inevitably, the jealous man went too far and succeeded only in toppling the marble edifice and crushing himself to death. As was the custom, the offending statue of Theagenes was brought to court, failed to enter a plea, was found guilty of murder, and punished by drowning.

4,493; Number of winners ridden by L Piggott. The greatest judge of other people's horses.

**THOMAS, MICKEY:** A colourful character, he was once stabbed in the arse by a cuckolded husband at 4 a.m. as he was going about his business in the back of a Volkswagen.

Ritchie Barker, his manager at Stoke City, says, 'He could be up all night in London, sleep in the Chelsea boot room, drive up to Stoke for a quarter to ten and still lead the cross-country in training.'

**Person he Would Most Like to Meet:** Pope John Paul II
**Favourite Food:** Corn Flakes
**Best Film:** *The Texas Chainsaw Massacre*

**THOMPSON, PHIL:** 'Phil Thompson has my number.' Alistair Campbell.

**THOUGHT FOR THE DAY:** Geoffrey Mortlake really did once say the following on Thought for the Day: 'It is entirely natural that as we struggle to comprehend and come to terms with what happened in Croatia there should be first confusion and then anger. What is important is that as true believers we direct our ire at the right targets.

The crisis of faith that has afflicted our football team is not the fault of the blessed Swede (whose book *Quarter-Final: My Autobiography* by Sven-Göran Eriksson and Geoffrey Mortlake will shortly be available in all bookshops) nor his disciple Hapless Mac, but of those who peddle the evil that is celebrity.

Here I stand and point the finger at the Pharisees in the press who have worshipped and elevated the WAGS. How is the boy Rooney meant to hold his head up high when fiancée Colleen is spilling the beans about their private life in best-selling women's weekly *Closer*? How is Crouchy going to walk tall when he is being shrivelled by the antics of his, and so many others', girlfriend? What is Lamps to make of the revelations that his wife drinks more than John Terry?

Enough already. We are being undermined from within. For the good of this once great nation (1966), let's get behind our boys and say nothing about their girls. Let's have a year's silence on this one. Amen.'

**THRING, THE BROTHERS:** The elder Thring was headmaster of Uppingham and given to delivering sermons entitled 'Death, and Death, and Death'. The younger Thring was the first person to attempt to codify what he called 'The Simplest Game' in just eleven rules. What is The Simplest Game? Football. And what are the Rules?! When they were codified as the Cambridge Rules (*c.* 1856) there were 11 as follows:

*The Laws of the University Foot Ball Club*

1. This club shall be called the University Foot Ball Club.

2. At the commencement of the play, the ball shall be kicked off from the middle of the ground: after every goal there shall be a kick-off in the same way.

3. After a goal, the losing side shall kick off; the sides changing goals, unless a previous arrangement be made to the contrary.

4. The ball is out when it has passed the line of the flag-posts on either side of the ground, in which case it shall be thrown in straight.

5. The ball is behind when it has passed the goal on either side of it.

6. When the ball is behind it shall be brought forward at the place where it left the ground, not more than ten paces, and kicked off.

7. Goal is when the ball is kicked through the flag-posts and under the string.

8. When a player catches the ball directly from the foot, he may kick it as he can without running with it. In no other case may the ball be touched with the hands, except to stop it.

9. If the ball has passed a player, and has come from the direction of his own goal, he may not touch it till the other side have kicked it, unless there are more than three of the other side before him. No player is allowed to loiter between the ball and the adversaries' goal.

10. In no case is holding a player, pushing with the hands, or tripping up allowed. Any player may prevent another from getting to the ball by any means consistent with the above rules.

11. Every match shall be decided by a majority of goals.

**TODD, LEE:** A striker for Sunday League team Cross Farm Park Celtic, he may well hold the record for the quickest dismissal. At the start of a game, as is traditional, the referee blew his whistle. Todd, who may have been severely hung over said: 'Fuck me, that was loud!' And was sent off, after two seconds.

**TRUEMAN, FRED:** Only Test cricketer to be consulted by the Government about invasion of Suez. Something of an acquired taste as an analyst, he was generally agreed to be at his best when rain stopped play. Only man to predict a Tory majority of over a hundred in the 1997 General Election.

**Test Match Record –**

| | |
|---|---|
| **Runs Scored:** 981 | **Wickets:** 307 |
| **Batting Av:** 13.81 | **Bowling Av:** 21.57 |
| **100s/50s:** 0/0 | **5 Wickets in innings:** 17 |
| **Top Score:** 39 | **10 Wickets in innings:** 3 |
| **Balls Bowled:** 15178 | **Best Bowling:** 8–31. |

One: The number of free kicks David Beckham scored in his last season at Manchester United (out of 19).

**TRYGGVASON, KING OLAF:** Renowned for being able to throw two javelins at once, without falling flat on his face, and adept at catching his opponent's javelin in flight.

**TYSON, MIKE:** Has had more dogs named after him than anyone on the planet.

**Wins:** 50
**Wins by KO:** 44
**Losses:** 6
**Draws:** 0
**No Contest:** 2
**Number of Appearances as a Referee on World Wrestling Foundation:** 1

# *Fighting Talk* Award for Worst Kit

And the nominations are:

1. ### JORGE CAMPOS'S GOALKEEPING SHIRTS
   'I've been looking for new kitchen curtains for a long time,' said former Norway keeper Erik Thorstvedt after exchanging jerseys at the 1994 World Cup. 'Growing up surfing in Acapulco influenced me,' said Campos.

2. ### KIRK STEVENS'S WHITE SUIT
   'I only wore the white suit as my black one was dirty, but after that I couldn't wear anything else as people expected it,' says Kirk who managed, for a while, to combine a successful snooker career with a burgeoning coke problem before deciding to jettison the snooker.

   Wayne Hemingway says: 'When I saw this picture I had no idea who he was but I wrote down "Can only be a snooker player." He is? I'm not surprised. It's so bad that ironic fashion types would consider it cool. He had a cocaine problem? Well, it's probably very sensible to wear a white suit if you have a coke problem.'

3. ### THE 1999 USA RYDER CUP TEAM
   Arguably the most sepia piece of sports clothing ever worn. It was Captain Ben Crenshaw's inspired decision to demand

that his team wear them for the final day's play at Brookline. The burgundy and cream shirts were decorated with pictures of past Ryder Cup-winning teams. A design feature which helpfully reminded the players what sporting competition they were playing in. Asked why his team had failed to wear something similar, European captain Mark James paused before saying 'I guess we missed out on that.'

Hemingway says: 'I don't have a problem with this at all. Hugh Hefner has a fantastic *Playboy* range of shirts out at the moment very similar to this – except with naked centrefolds on them, instead of old golfers. You can buy them on *Playboy's* website. Las Vegas stores are full of shirts like this, they're very in just now. It's very *Sopranos*. I think golf gear in general is very cool.'

And the winners are those God-fearing golfers.

# Homework

Mark the following examples of homework and see if you can do better . . .

Wayne Rooney had revealed that he's a fan of the musical *Oliver*, so can we have your suggestions for sports stars who might appear in a West End musical production?

- Given his undeniable creepiness and his policy of buying up young talent from around Europe for next to nothing, surely Arsène Wenger would make a cracking Child Catcher in *Chitty Chitty Bang Bang* . . . think about it . . .

- Dennis Wise and Gus Poyet in *Little Shop of Horrors*. Wise as the shop assistant and Poyet as his angry, foul mouthed, blood craving plant.

- Arsène Wenger and Alex Ferguson: *Les Misérables*.

- José Mourinho as Oliver. OK you gave me £200m but can I have some more?

DEFEND THE INDEFENSIBLE
Porn barons should be exempt from bung enquiries.

*or*

It's all true, we really can't throw. (to the first lady of *Fighting Talk*, Eleanor Oldroyd).

QUESTION
**Ice-skating:** are you a Harding man or a Kerrigan man?

**Tonya Harding:** Daughter of an alcoholic mother and unmotivated father. Asthmatic. Twice US Champion and first woman to perform a triple Axel. Harshly implicated in kneecapping attempt on rival during warm-ups for 1994 US figure-skating Championships. Moved sideways into the world of nude Internet celebrity. And boxing (career record 3-3-0).

**Kerrigan:** Well spoken with a blind mother. Tomboy. Pretty much unknown before being clubbed in knee. 'Whyyyy?' 'Whyyyy?' Finished 2nd in 1994 Olympics and left early for publicity parade at Walt Disney World. Small part in Will Ferrell vehicle *Blades of Glory*.

(Extra marks will be awarded for stick drawing of a triple Axel being performed.)

# Stats

LOWEST POPULATED COUNTRIES' SUCCESS AT OLYMPIC
GAMES AS A PROPORTION OF GROSS DOMESTIC PRODUCT
(GDP) PER CAPITA ($)

| Country | Population | Total Gold | Total Silver | Total Bronze | Total Medals |
|---|---|---|---|---|---|
| Bermuda | 65,000 | | | 1 | 1 |
| US Virgin Islands | 111,000 | | 1 | | 1 |
| Netherlands Antilles | 192,000 | | 1 | | 1 |
| Barbados | 294,000 | | | 1 | 1 |
| Iceland | 316,252 | | 1 | 2 | 3 |
| Bahamas | 331,000 | 3 | 2 | 3 | 8 |
| Suriname | 458,000 | 1 | | 1 | 2 |
| Guyana | 738,000 | | | 1 | 1 |
| Djibouti | 833,000 | | | 1 | 1 |
| Qatar | 841,000 | | | 2 | 2 |

| | GDP Per Capita ($) | Medals as a % of GDP Per Capita |
|---|---|---|
| Bermuda | 69,900 | 0.0014 |
| US Virgin Islands | 14,500 | 0.0069 |
| Netherlands Antilles | 16,000 | 0.0063 |
| Barbados | 19,700 | 0.0051 |
| Iceland | 39,400 | 0.0076 |
| Bahamas | 22,700 | 0.0352 |
| Suriname | 7800 | 0.0256 |

| Guyana | 5300 | 0.0189 |
| Djibouti | 1000 | 0.1000 |
| Qatar | 75,900 | 0.0026 |

The smallest countries by size of population (looking solely at those countries with less than 1 million population) that have competed at the Olympic Games since 1952 and have achieved medals in these Olympics up to 2004, and divided the total number of medals achieved by the current GDP per capita to obtain the number of medals as a percentage of GDP per capita.

Despite the fact that Bahamas has the best record in the Olympics in terms of medals out of the recorded economies, Djibouti has the highest medals as a percentage of GDP per capita as it has a very low level of GDP. As Iceland has a higher GDP than most of these countries, despite the fact that it has won 3 medals in total it still ranks quite low in terms of medals as a percentage of GDP per capita.

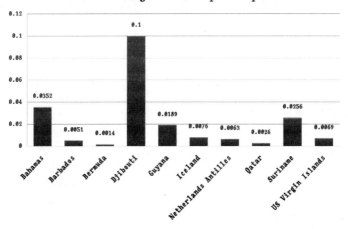

Lowest Populated Countries Medals Success at the Olympics since 1952 as a Percentage of GDP per Capita

# U

**UNDERDOGS:** On each of the three occasions they have won the World Cup the Germans have been the underdogs.

In 1954 when the country didn't even have a nationwide league, and after they had lost 8–3 to Hungary in the group stage, and despite being two down within ten minutes against the same opponents in the final, they won 3–2.

In 1974, they humiliatingly lost the only game they would ever play against East Germany in the group stage, went 1–0 down to Holland in the first minute of the final, and won 2–1.

In 1990, they beat Maradona's Argentina in the most boring final ever contested.

**UNDER-RATED:** By his own estimation the BBC's Mark Bright is under-rated.

Thirteen: The number of times Phil DeFreitas was dropped by England. 'You have a feeling every time that something's going to happen to you,' he says. 'You can sense it by people's body language or attitude towards you. People were careful of what they said or what they did, which means they knew before you knew. All through my career I knew exactly when I was going to be dropped. If we've lost a Test and I've got 2 wickets and 20 runs I knew I'd be dropped. I was a scapegoat.'

**Stats:**
**Bowled** more than 120,000 overs
**Took** over 1,000 wickets
**Scored** over 10,000 runs

**UNDERSTANDING CRICKET:** 'I am going to make a promise to the Foreign Minister right now and that is that I will even try to understand cricket.' US Secretary of State Condoleeza Rice.

**UNDER THE CARPET:** 'The Republicans in the USA manipulate public opinion and brush the delicate questions under the carpet. Decisions in America are based solely on how much money will come out of it, and not on the questions of how much health, morals and the environment might suffer as a result.' Martina Navratilova.

**UNSURE ABOUT GETTING BACK UP:** 'My toenails were aching. I took a bunch of pills and I made it and I feel fine now. I'm still aching. I'm glad I did the 18 holes. I sat down a couple of times and I wasn't sure I'd get back up.' Arnie Palmer on his final round.

**UNTERMENSCH:** 'I am confident you will defeat the *untermensch*.' The message wired by Adolf Hitler to Max Schmeling before he was knocked out in the first round by Joe Louis.

**URINATION:**

1. Par Zetterberg, denying reports he'd stormed off the Anderlecht bench after a row with coach Hugo Broos said, 'I was not angry with him – I just had to urinate. I told Broos I

was not mad at him. What else could I do? Pee on the bench? Maybe I should bring a cup with me next time. Maybe next time it will be in the newspaper when I fart on the bench. Jesus.'

2. Norwegian goalkeeper Olav Fiske, who was seen drinking several pints of water before his side's cup-tie, found himself in trouble when the game went into extra time. With the ball upfield he rushed to the touchline to relieve himself, only to watch in horror – midstream – as opposition striker Tor Oddvar Torve lobbed the ball 40 yards into the net. The match finished 1–0.

# *Fighting Talk* Baftas II

## BEST CHILDREN'S SPORTS PROGRAMME: *WE ARE THE CHAMPIONS*

A school sports day meets *Jeux Sans Frontières* with Ron Pickering in the commentary booth. Every week three teams of kids from unlikely sounding schools would muck around outside before 'heading inside for the pool' where the serious action would begin. Every renewal would end with Ron Pickering commanding, 'Away you go!' and the children leaping into the water quicker than Malcolm Allison when he spotted troubled vicar's daughter Fiona Richmond in the club Jacuzzi.

Disappointingly, not a single contestant went on to represent their country at any sport, least of all swimming.

## LIFETIME ACHIEVEMENT AWARD: *INDOOR LEAGUE*

The greatest sports programme ever broadcast. It attracted an audience of eight million. It featured hitherto unbroadcast (able) sports – Darts, Skittles, Shove Ha'Penny, Table Football. It was presented by Fred Trueman. And, uniquely in sports broadcasting history, he signed off each show with a wink and a 'I'll si' thee . . .'

Over to Sid Waddell to collect the award. 'It made stars of pubbers and scrubbers, potters and slotters, 'pottin', slottin', tossin' and bossin'. They were an odd bunch. One of them was a cowboy from Scarborough who had personalised ha'pennys in his holster and went by the name of Buffalo Bill.'

'We thought we had seen it all, but then there was the Leaning Tower of Shoreditch, Ron Church – 6ft 4in with snaggle teeth in a moth-eaten cardigan – he'd down four pints before he threw a practice dart.'

'There was this arm wrestler from Kensington dressed like Marlon Brando in *The Wild One*,' says Sid, gearing up another anecdote. 'He had very pale skin, wore a leather hat and sent in some pictures of himself on a bike, Mark Sinclair-Scott from Kensington. Anyway, he wins the arm wrestling and two weeks later Fred came in to do the links. And the night before he had just launched his career as a comedian and played the Fiesta in Middlesbrough and been up until three in the morning. Now it was ten the next morning and he had to have a pint in his hands for continuity and all the guy had was a 16 pack of Newcastle Brown Ale. The line Fred had to say was, "He's Mark Sinclair-Scott and he's the Narcissus of the Knotted Knuckles". Fred has had four pints of continuity and he says, "He's Mark Sinclair-Scott and he's the Nancy Boy with the Knotted Knuckles."'

# Homework

Mark the following examples of homework and see if you can do better . . .

Hello, can we please have some books that sports people should be reading?

- Kevin Keegan – *Great Expectations*.

- Andy Murray should read the big book of jokes then maybe the guy would crack a smile.

- Stan Collymore – *The Curious Incident of the Dog in the Night-time*.

DEFEND THE INDEFENSIBLE
Forget the Olympic Torch, let's set the Dalai Lama on fire and send him around the world.

*or*

I thought the questions today were going to be all about shopping, *OK* and *Desperate Housewives*. Like many women I know nothing about sport (to Hazel Irvine).

QUESTION
**Barry Bonds:** Black or white? Reconcile the comments by two US sports journalists and arrive at a conclusion with which Trevor Brooking would be comfortable.

'Bonds's records should stay in the record books. With a little syringe next to every one,' writes *Sports Illustrated* columnist Rick Reilly in *Hate Mail from Cheerleaders and Other Adventures from the Life of Reilly* (foreword kindly provided by Lance Armstrong).

'He is the Sean Penn of Major League Baseball, a Sean Penn in a Tom Hanks world,' writes Dave Zirin. 'Bonds has always been surly towards the media and always disliked Mr Reilly and Reilly returned the favour. Reilly wants to be as big a star as the athletes and when they don't treat him like that he becomes resentful. There is no love at the end of this rainbow. Like Jack Johnson, Bonds has an unforgivable blackness. One of the reasons he wants to break it is a big F you to everyone who doesn't want him to.'

# Stats

## PREMIERSHIP AVERAGE SEASON TICKET PRICES

| Team | Highest Price (£) | Lowest Price (£) | Average Price (£) |
|---|---|---|---|
| Celtic | 575 | 440 | 507.50 |
| Rangers | 612 | 298 | 455.00 |
| Bayern Munich | 473.46 | 94.72 | 284.09 |
| AC Milan | 1421.46 | 102.71 | 762.09 |
| Juventus | 1410.56 | 105.77 | 758.17 |

| Team | Average Price (£) | Team | Average Price (£) |
|---|---|---|---|
| Celtic | 507.50 | Fulham | 524.0 |
| Rangers | 455.00 | Liverpool | 675.0 |
| Bayern Munich | 284.09 | Man City | 461.0 |
| AC Milan | 762.09 | Man Utd | 655.5 |
| Juventus | 758.17 | Middlesbrough | 470.0 |
| Arsenal | 1367.5 | Newcastle Utd | 715.0 |
| Aston Villa | 337.5 | Portsmouth | 685.0 |
| Birmingham | 517.5 | Sunderland | 602.5 |
| Blackburn | 324.0 | Reading | 580.0 |
| Bolton | 399.0 | Tottenham | 1064.5 |
| Chelsea | 840.0 | West Ham | 722.5 |
| Derby | 365.0 | Wigan | 250.0 |
| Everton | 523.5 | | |

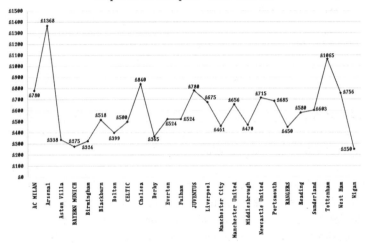

Premiership Average Season Ticket Prices
compared to European Clubs 2007-08

AC MILAN £780
Arsenal £1368
Aston Villa £338
BAYERN MUNICH £275
Birmingham £324
Blackburn £518
Bolton £399
CELTIC £500
Chelsea £840
Derby £365
Everton £524
Fulham £524
JUVENTUS £780
Liverpool £675
Manchester City £461
Manchester United £656
Middlesbrough £470
Newcastle United £715
Portsmouth £685
RANGERS £450
Reading £580
Sunderland £603
Tottenham £1065
West Ham £756
Wigan £250

**VACUUM, FILLED A:** 'It's hard to believe what human beings have done in the world. Golf played a prominent role and filled a vacuum that might have existed.' Gary Player.

**VAN DER SAR, EDWIN:** Manchester United's Edwin van der Sar's favourite holiday destination. 'I like Italy very much. I like the food, the culture and the nice weather of course.' His favourite film is *The Godfather* series. 'They are classics.' He meets famous people 'Quite a lot, but I'm not into all that stuff. I did meet Prince Harry two years ago at a restaurant in southwest London. I had a very nice conversation with him for a couple of hours. That was a good experience.' At home he reads the *Daily Mail*. And if he wasn't a footballer he thinks he would like to be 'a guy who works in or owns a sports store – that idea has always interested me.'

**VEGETABLE SOUP:** The favourite food of Poland's Kazimierz Denya. He doesn't own a car.

*£388,000, £444,000, £492,000*
*West Ham's chairman Terence Brown once really said, 'I hope that, in due course, all our supporters will understand the need for the belt-tightening which is taking place. We cannot gamble with 107 years of hard-earned history.' Brown's salary in:*
*2001: £388k;*
*2002: £444k;*
*2003: £492k, plus pension and chauffeured car. He was the second-highest paid chairman in football, after Freddie Shepherd. And Shepherd doesn't count because of his excessive outgoings (see* News of the World *passim)*

**VELVET THRONES:** 'You could say we've got a liking for "subtle-over-the-top",' said David Beckham, as he and Victoria chose the gilt and velvet thrones for their wedding bash.

**VENABLES, TERRY:** Was initially earmarked to present *The Apprentice*. The winner would be offered two days a week on his market stall. Sadly, a late format change cleared the way for his rival A Sugar Esq.

> **Club Apps:** 510 **Goals:** 64
> **England Apps:** 2 **Goals:** 0
> **Managed:** Crystal Place, QPR, Barcelona, Tottenham Hotspur, England, Australia, Crystal Palace, Middlesbrough, Leeds, England (Assistant Manager)
> **The only football manager to make it on to the Booker long list with** *They Used to Play on Grass.*

**VERY DIFFERENT REASONS:** Arguably the greatest picture caption ever to appear in *Shoot!* was 'Neil (Orr) is a big fan of Olivia Newton-John (far left) and Arnold Mühren (right) – but for very different reasons!'

**VIALLI, GIANLUCA:** Said about the Italian practice of *furbo*: 'When an opponent won a penalty against us by diving or making a meal of slight contact, the attitude among players and coaches wasn't to condemn him for cheating but to point the finger at our own defenders for allowing it to happen. "He was clever!" we were told. "He tricked you and he tricked the referee." We were engaging in footballing realpolitik.'

**Club Apps:** 656 **Goals:** 225
**Italy Apps:** 59 **Goals:** 16
**Managed:** Chelsea, Watford
**Number of Suits Owned:** 783 (84 are from Comme des Garçons)
**The best-dressed man ever to lead out a team at Wembley.**

**VICARIOUS LIVING:** 'I don't live vicariously through Crystal Palace, Crystal Palace live vicariously through me.' Simon Jordan.

**VICK, MICHAEL:** Atlanta Falcons quarterback serving a 23-month prison sentence for criminal conspiracy resulting from felonious dog fighting. Following discovery in April 2007 of extensive facilities used for dog fighting at his 15-acre property near Smithfield, Virginia, Vick and three other men were convicted on federal felony charges related to his involvement with an illegal interstate dog fighting ring known as Bad Newz Kennels. On 10 December 2007, Vick was sentenced to 23 months in federal prison, to be followed by three years of supervised probation. All for the love of a good dog.

**VIMTO, HOT:** 'It's delicious,' says Blackburn's Jason Roberts.

**VINE, DAVID:** Has never skied in his life, yet you would never have known from his consummate presentation of *Ski Sunday*.

# The *Fighting Talk* Award for Greatest Sporting Cold War Confrontation

And the nominations are:

### 1. ALEXANDER KARELIN *v* RULON GARDNER (SYDNEY 2000)

The Cold War had been over for a decade but there remained the little matter of the Greco-Roman 130kg + Olympic gold to resolve. In the red corner, Alexander Karelin attempting a Redgravian fifth consecutive Olympic gold. Karelin plays chess, likes ballet and opera, writes poetry, reads Nabokov and Bulgakov and once carried a fridge back from the shop and, unassisted, lugged it up to the kitchen of his 8th floor flat. In the blue corner, Rulon Gardner, the youngest of nine children raised by Mormon parents on an isolated dairy farm in Scar Valley, Wyoming. He is a fat man, inside whom is an even fatter man trying to get out. Astonishingly, the phenomenally lardy farm boy triumphs on a technicality. The longest streak in individual sport is ended by a ball of fat. The metaphors remain obvious to all.

### 2. ROCKY BALBOA *v* CAPTAIN IVAN DRAGO (CHRISTMAS DAY 1985, MOSCOW)

The final Cold War confrontation. Upset by seeing old sparring partner Apollo Creed literally battered to death by

Drago and the Russian's lack of remorse ('if he dies, he dies'), Rocky Balboa stirs himself one more time and gets his arse to Moscow in search of revenge. The fight, completely unbelievably, is not sanctioned by any boxing body.

Drago is implied to be taking anabolic steroids, Stallone, meanwhile . . .. Rocky wins by a knockout in the 15th. He is cheered to the rafters by the Soviet crowd. Emboldened, he turns to the men in the Politburo seats and says, 'if I can change . . . and you can change . . . everyone can change!' Four years later the Berlin Wall came down.

### 3. USA *v* SOVIET UNION (ICE HOCKEY SEMI-FINAL, LAKE PLACID, 1980)

A bunch of amateur college boys facing up to the might of the Soviet ice hockey machine – there could only be one winner. With ten minutes remaining the score is 3–3 when Mike Eruzione speeds past a couple of bamboozled Soviet defenders and scores what proves to be the winner. At the end, Communist Party officials enter the Soviet locker room and say, 'You guys just made one of the biggest mistakes of your lives. Ten years from now, 20 years, everyone will remember this game.' It has been described as a 'defining moment in American culture' and 'the greatest sports event of the 20th century' (both quotes coming from Americans).

And the winner is Rocky Balboa, every time.

# Homework

Mark the following examples of homework and see if you can do better . . .

A pundit has described their local politician as wine, 'bottles early, distinctly fishy and definitely corked', so can I have your descriptions of sports people or teams as a drink?

- Phil Thompson, European Cup-winning Liverpool defender and pundit – a classy red with a remarkable nose.

- Newcastle United as a drink would be absinthe, as they're both addictive, leave their consumers with delirium and romantic views of grandeur. Over-consumption can lead to blindness – particularly to the limitations of the team.

- Frank Lampard – Southern Comfort and lemonade – from the south, a bit camp, might taste nice but pretty useless!

- Glen Roeder as a warm, flat beer . . . . . . with a fly in it. Uncharismatic and you wouldn't want to touch it with a barge pole!

- Carlos Tevez – A surprisingly nice bottle of wine bought on the cheap and smuggled through customs.

DEFEND THE INDEFENSIBLE
The rugby World Cup would have been more entertaining if one of the team coaches had died under suspicious circumstances

*or*

Now that Britney Spears is single again I think I might have a go
(to John Rawling).

QUESTION
Arbitrate on the following pub argument:

**Richard 'I dwell in the future' Scudamore** (former advertising man
and assistant referee, currently head of the Premier League) said of
Michel Platini's ideas that 'they don't rise much above the view of
people in the corner of the pub.' Before going on to say, 'This is
where the marketer in me comes out . . . it's all about making sure
the pie gets bigger all the time.'

**Michel Platini:** (most elegant footballer of his generation and a
chain-smoker) replied, 'We are the guardians of European football.
Our role is to protect the game from business, this is my
philosophy; Scudamore's job is to make more business for the club
owners, the US businessmen buying your clubs today. They want to
make money. I say. "Take care".'

# Stats

## PREMIERSHIP SEASON TICKETS PER CLUB AS A PROPORTION OF LOCAL AUTHORITY WAGES 2007-08

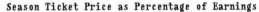

Season Ticket Price as Percentage of Earnings

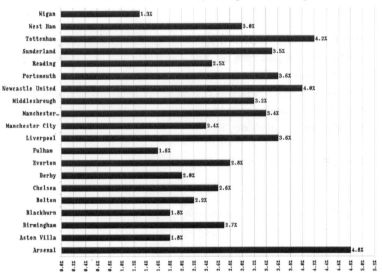

*Wages Source: 'Annual Survey of Earnings and Hours 2007'*
Local authority median wage taken for each club and average season ticket price measured as a proportion of this wage.

**WALKING THE DOG:** 'If you want a really long career you have to find a way of switching off. I do it when I'm out walking my dog, Alex Ferguson got into horses, others get into wine. Some players like going shopping, which is not my scene. A lot of them turn to golf. I tried it, didn't like it. I have got to walk. If I couldn't I'd be in a padded cell by now.' Roy Keane.

**WATER:** Wigan's Mario Melchiot 'loves simple, still water.'

90% to go: 'There's 6,000 million people in the world, and only 600 million have ever heard of snooker. That means we've got another ninety per cent to go.' Barry Hearn.

**WATNEY'S CUP:** When men were men and football was football, the Watney's Cup symbolised all that was right about the game. A glorious tournament open only to the highest scoring team in each Division which, despite 'banging in goals for fun', hadn't actually won a trophy. Created to advertise the benefits of the remarkable 'Party 7'.

**WEAH, GEORGE:** Ran for Liberian President in 2005, securing most votes in the first ballot but not securing the overall majority needed; in a run-off vote he lost to former finance minister Ellen Johnson-Sirleaf who became the first elected female president in Africa.

Club Apps: 504 Goals: 223
Liberia Apps: 60 Goals: 22

**WEARING NIKE:** 'You need comfortable shoes. I like the Adidas shoe, but if someone wants to wear Nike, I won't hold them back.' Melissa Lehman, explaining *The Stepford Wives*' shoe strategy at the 2006 Ryder Cup.

**WEARING SOMETHING NEW:** 'I could relate to him. He was someone I followed. Every day he would come out wearing something new, something different.' Ian Poulter on Payne Stewart.

**WEBSITE STILL BUSY:** 'It's not over till it's over. I'm still undefeated, still learning, still improving, it's all there in front of me to be achieved . . . I think there's still a story in Audley Harrison. My website's still busy.'

**WEGERLE, ROY:** It's half time away at Man City, Rangers have been dismal and Ian Holloway is bawling out Roy Wegerle.
'How dare you say that to Roy Wegerle?' says captain Alan McDonald.
'Fuck off!' says Holloway.
'Sometimes it's just meant to be, Ollie,' says Wegerle.

Years taken to record first Test series victory: South Africa 17 years, India 20 years, New Zealand 40 years.

**WEIGHT CLAUSE:** 'For instance, Fatty Arbuckle, Neil Ruddock, wanted to sign. And Harry Redknapp told me to make sure I had a weight clause in his contract. Ninety-eight kilos, or whatever. And if he's over that then fine him 10% of his wages. That is the only way to ensure you get a fit and focused Ruddock. Now this is the kind of thing best explained by one football man to another, not by a new chairman, but Steve [Coppell] wasn't interested. He was so negative he interfered with the signal strength on my phone.' Simon Jordan.

**WELCH, RAQUEL:** 'She was over promoting a film and Sir Richard Attenborough brought her along and she said she wanted to meet Peter Osgood. Terry O'Neill who was her photographer was also my photographer at the time. She was gorgeous, lovely, stunning.' Peter Osgood.

**WELSBY, ELTON:** Who was he? What did he do? Where did he go? (see also Tony Gubba).

**WICKET-KEEPERS:** The following commentary really did accompany Sky's coverage of India *v* Zimbabwe:

> **Sunny Gavaskar:** Wicket-keepers make great lovers.
> **Greg Chappell:** Why's that, Sunny?
> **S.G:** Because they go up at the slightest opportunity.
> **G.C:** The keepers I've known – Ian Healy, Rodney Marsh, Barry Jarman – spent most of their time off the field taking refreshment.
> **S.G:** And why do you think they wanted all that refreshment?
> **G.C:** Why's that, Sunny?
> **S.G:** To lubricate themselves.
> **G.C:** (stomping out) I've never been so relieved to leave a commentary booth in all my life.

**WILDERSTEIN, ALEC:** Arguably the most bad-tempered horse owner of his generation. After Dominique Boeuf had failed to win the Coronation Cup on Vallée Enchantée, Wildenstein was asked if he had been a mite unlucky and replied: 'We weren't unlucky. She was ridden by an asshole who didn't follow instructions.' Moments later, the 'arsehole' was downsized. After Godolphin's Papineau had beaten Wildenstein's Westerner to win the Ascot Gold Cup, he looked over at the winner's enclosure and said, 'The dope-testing machine must be broken.'

Over the years he has dispensed with the services of, inter alia, Lester Piggott and Pat Eddery. He has also dispensed with one wife, Jocelyne, after a curious marriage. For a while everything went swimmingly. He gave her a pet monkey, she gave him two children. Around about fifty they found a shared hobby in plastic surgery. The hobby getting somewhat out of control when Jocelyne asked her plastic surgeon to transform her into one of the giant cats that Alec loved so much. It is possible the surgeon did too good a job. At the divorce Wildenstein claimed he 'couldn't even recognise my own wife up close'. Matters became increasingly petty when he 'reduced her further use of their jet, and she was forced to remain in isolation in New York, without the solace of her monkey – but just around the corner from her plastic surgeon.' At the trial she claimed to need seven staff because she literally couldn't make toast. At its conclusion, 'The Bride of Wildenstein' was awarded many millions but had to pick up the tab for any further plastic surgery she might want. She was also awarded a sum by the judge to allow her to buy a microwave.

> When Sachin Tendulkar bats against Pakistan the television audience in India alone exceeds the combined population of Europe.

**WILLEY, PETER:** The only cricketer to defeat Ian Botham at arm wrestling. After he had won, Botham taunted him by asking 'How many Test wickets have you got?' Willey said, 'Enough,' challenged Both to another contest, and won again.

**WILSON, JOCKY:** Scottish darts player of the 1970s who was so drunk he didn't notice he'd lost all his teeth. Once missed when attempting to shake hands with an opponent after a game in a pub in Stoke and ended up in the pit with the drum kit.

> **BDO World Champion:** 1982 and 1989
> **BBC2 Bullseye Darts Championship winner:** 1980, 1981
> **Favourite Food:** Neeps

**WIMBLEDON, SECOND WEEK OF:** For a British women's tennis player to make it into the second week of Wimbledon normally requires not only that it rains from Monday to Friday but also that she receives the luck of the draw. The last player to achieve the feat was Sam Smith in 1998.

**WINNING:** 'A good habit to get into.' Alan Shearer.

**WISDEN APOLOGY:** 'Note: Last year the obituary of GA Wheatley, who ran the cricket at Uppingham School for 32 years, stated that "late in life and to general surprise he married one of the matrons". This is untrue, and Wisden apologises to Dr and Mrs Wheatley's family and friends for the offence it caused. Garth Wheatley married at 29; Mrs Wheatley, whom he met on a cricket tour in Ireland, was 20 at the time and was never a matron at the school.'

'3.00 p.m. prompt'. Professor AJ Ayer was in the habit of starting his football match reports for the *Observer* with: 'The match kicked off at 3.00 p.m. prompt.'

**WOOLF, VIRGINIA:** 'It is no coincidence that the best of Mr Lardner's stories are about games, for one may guess that Mr Lardner's interest in games has solved one of the most difficult problems of the American writer; it has given him a clue, a centre, a meeting place for the divers activities of people whom a vast continent isolates, whom no tradition controls. Games give him what society gives his English brother.'

**WORLD'S STRONGEST MAN:** The Tour de France without the hypocrisy, athletics without the inexplicable absences from competition. It is the fastest growing sport in Eastern Europe. As with the World Wrestling Federation (WWF), props are fundamental to World's Strongest Man (WSM). Obviously, the 'strong men' (otherwise known as actors) do not actually lift a Stone of Asia weighing x kilos, or whatever, rather they play with a block of polystyrene painted battleship grey. The grand finale in which five so-called Atlas Stones weighing x+y kilos must be placed on a pedestal in actuality involves much faux grunting and groaning and the hefting of five giant Maltesers. 'That's not stone, it's honeycomb,' Magnus ver Magnusson once said, off-camera.

# The *Fighting Talk* Tribute for Worst Player Selection

1. **THE PORTLAND TRAIL BLAZERS:** In 1984 the Blazers decided to go with the 7ft 1in Sam Bowie out of Kentucky in the Basketball Draft pick rather than, for instance, Michael Jordan. Bowie 'blazed a trail in the trainer's room sitting out 189 games in his first four seasons' and retired shortly thereafter. Jordan fared rather better. Blighted throughout his sort of career by comparisons with Jordan, Bowie too planned a comeback at 40 after resigning as basketball analyst for the University of Kentucky Radio Network. 'At one point some folks out there obviously felt he was a better player than Michael,' said a member of Bowie's small posse who requested that his name not be used. 'He'd like to think that some people out there still feel that way.' And perhaps they did.

2. **THE MCC:** Given that Basil D'Oliveira had scored 158 not out in an Ashes-clinching defeat of the Australians at the Oval, he had good reason to hope he might be selected for the tour to South Africa in 1968. Dream on. He was omitted for 'cricketing reasons'. South African Prime Minister Vorster had told Alec Douglas-Hume and Lord Cobham that the selection of D'Oliveira would lead to the tour's cancellation

being an irrelevant co-incidence. The MCC President at the time was Arthur Gilligan, ex-member of the British Union of Fascists and author of *The Spirit of Fascism and Cricket Tours*. As it turned out, Tom Cartwright was injured, D'Oliveira, not before time, selected, and Vorster, as he had threatened to do, cancelled the tour. It was the last time the MCC picked the England team.

And the winner. The MCC, every time.

# Homework

Mark the following examples of homework and see if you can do better . . .

Can you suggest some sports people who could appear in Bond movies please?

- Bond characters – Teddy Sheringham as Pussy Galore.

- Craig Bellamy could play Nick-Nack, a vicious homicidal dwarf who ought to be found stuffed in a suitcase.

- He's smooth, suave. He does everything with grace and makes it look easy in the process. Every man hates him out of jealousy, but he is so cool that you secretly want to be him. Thierry Henry is the James Bond of football.

DEFEND THE INDEFENSIBLE
The women's World Cup would be taken more seriously if the players didn't wear bras.

*or*

I'd encourage my missus to take steroids if they made her even half as cute as Marion Jones.

ESSAY
**History:** Discuss the legacy of those two super-powers of 10th-century sport the Irish and the Norse, giving particular emphasis to differences between the two (e.g. the Irish liked horse-racing, while the Vikings liked horse-baiting. A lifestyle choice traditionally explained by the fact that the Irish loved a gamble

while the Vikings loved satire). Do not forget to mention the merger between the cultures which was an inevitable consequence of the Vikings, with their eye for a quick profit, having made a tiny fortune from trading Irish wives.

# Stats

## PREMIERSHIP CLUBS SEASON TICKET PRICES 2007–08

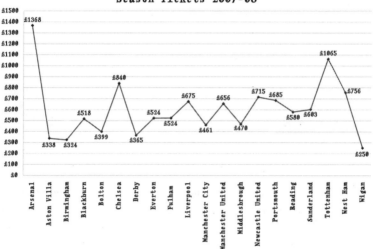

Average Price for Premiership
Season Tickets 2007-08

# X

*5,000 points: The highest score ever on* Fighting Talk *was achieved by Steve Bunce on 26 November 2005. Following numerous deductions by host Christian O'Connell for Bunce's petulance, Bunce's Any Other Business was a story about Bob Wilson for which O'Connell awarded 5,000 points. Bunce went on to win Defending the Indefensible.*

**X, CASSIUS:** After he was known as Cassius Clay and before he was known as Muhammad Ali he was, for a week, called Cassius X.

–900,000: The lowest score recorded was Steve Bunce's –900,000 (Season 3).

# Homework

Mark the following examples of homework and see if you can do better . . .

Robbie Savage was described this week as a human spark plug so we want sports people as something knocking about in your garage.

- Jonny Wilkinson is that bag of broken bits that you're sure will come in useful again one of these days.

- Nicolas Anelka is the exercise bike in the garage. You bought it from the guy next door who bought it from the guy over the road who bought it from the school who bought it from the vicar, who bought it from the health centre. You all paid too much for it thinking it would do you good but soon realise that either you weren't interested or it wasn't as good as you were told so you are looking round for the next mug to take it off your hands, at a profit if possible.

- Teddy Sheringham has got to be the classic car. a vintage performer that has had many owners and only gets a run out for an hour every Sunday.

- Phil Neville is a petrol can. You take it out hoping not to use it.

DEFEND THE INDEFENSIBLE
William Gallas's on-pitch sit down was a more moving protest than anything Gandhi and Mandela ever put together.

*or*

This programme was a farce last week when we had a woman presenting it (to first lady of *Fighting Talk*, Eleanor Oldroyd).

QUESTION
**Bull-fighting:** A wonderful way to take some exercise and meet the right sort of people.

*or*

Evil, vermin, scum. If there was any justice in the world it would be the bull-fighters who would be chased round the ring and poked with tiny swords.

Argue both sides against the middle.

# Stats

| Team | Average Price (£) |
| --- | --- |
| Accrington Stanley | 276.0 |
| Barnet | 332.5 |
| Bradford | 138.0 |
| Brentford | 350.0 |
| Bury | 220.0 |
| Chester | 285.0 |
| Chesterfield | 362.5 |
| Dagenham & Redbridge | 270.0 |
| Darlington | 304.0 |
| Grimsby | 323.0 |
| Hereford | 280.0 |
| Lincoln | 312.5 |
| Macclesfield | 252.0 |
| Mansfield | 310.0 |
| MK Dons | 442.5 |
| Morecombe | 247.0 |
| Notts County | 292.0 |
| Peterborough | 327.5 |
| Rochdale | 252.5 |
| Rotherham | 357.5 |
| Shrewsbury | 402.5 |
| Stockport | 273.0 |
| Wrexham | 287.5 |
| Wycombe | 292.5 |

# Average Price for League Two Season Tickets 2007-08

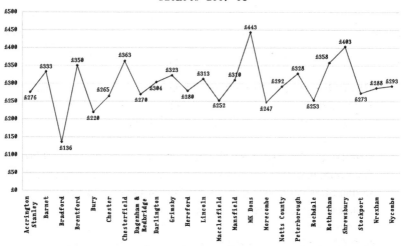

# Y

**YIELDING HIGH RETURNS:** 'Investing in property can yield high returns for the tennis pro, but make sure you do your homework first.' *iTennis Pros* in-house magazine.

**YOGHURT TO FINISH:** 'I've got more important things to think about than him. I've a yogurt to finish and the expiry date is today.' Gordon Strachan having become tired of mothering troubled Ecuadorian striker Agustin Delgado.

**YORKSHIRE ELECTRICITY CUP:** A competition in which Halifax were Kings. They won the first YEC with a 3–2 win at Rotherham (a.e.t). After the Cup took a two-year time out. They won the renewal with a 4–2 win at Bradford City. There were no other Yorkshire Electricity Cups. Halifax in the Electricity was as near as you could come to a perfect banker.

**YOUNG CLOUGH:** 'I like the look of Mourinho, there's a bit of the young Clough about him. For a start, he's good-looking and, like me, he doesn't believe in the star system. He's consumed with team spirit and discipline.' Brian Clough, just before he died.

434 and 5248: Kapil Dev took more Test wickets (434) than Richard Hadlee, Ian Botham and Imran Khan and he also scored more runs (5248) than any of them.

**YOUNG, PERCY M:** Friend of Edward Elgar, composer and one of the great unacknowledged football writers. He recommended that spectators 'memorise and use at discretion – if that is the right word' the following passage:

'Of all the blear-eyed nincompoops that ever appeared in spindle-shanks on the turf in the guise of a referee, the cachinnatory cough-drop who attempted the job on Saturday was the worst we have ever seen. His asinine imbecility was only equalled by his mountebank costume, and his general appearance and get-up reminded one more of a baked frog than a man. No worse tub-thumping, pot-bellied, jerry-built jackass ever tried to perform as a referee. His lugubrious tenebrousness and his monotonous squeaking on the whistle were a trial to the soul. Encased in a dull psychological envelopment of weird chaotic misunderstandings of the rules, he gyrated in a ludicrously painful manner up and down the field, and his addle-headed, flat-chested, splay-footed, cross-eyed, unkempt, unshaven, bow-legged, humpbacked, lop-eared, scraggy, imbecilic and idiotic decision when he rules Jones' second goal off-side, filled the audience, players and spectators alike, with disgust.'

# Homework

Mark the following examples of homework and see if you can do better . . .

Gordon Strachan said he would like 24's starring hero Jack Bauer in Celtic's back four. What other TV stars could lend a hand to the world of sport?

- Dale Winton for Wolves. He's already orange and would stiffen up the back four.

- Jade Goody for Chelsea just to give them that touch of class they so desperately need.

- Michael Jackson could possible join Liverpool if he wanted to get spanked at home by 11 kids (which he doesn't).

- It's surely got to be Liverpool's new central defensive partnership of Rick Waller and Michelle McManus, there's no way the beast could get through them.

DEFEND THE INDEFENSIBLE
The French are right. Horses aren't for racing, they're for eating.

*or*

I hold my hands up, the *Rumour Mill* was rubbish (to Steve Bunce, host of the *Rumour Mill*).

ESSAY
**Law:** It has been written of Ted Williams that 'he wished to be famous but had no interest in being a celebrity. What Ted Williams

wanted to be famous for was his hitting. He wanted everyone who cared about baseball to know that he was – as he believed and may well have been – the greatest pure hitter who ever lived. What he didn't want to do was to take on any of the effort off the baseball field involved in making this known. As an active player, Williams gave no interviews, signed no baseballs or photographs, chose not to be obliging in any way to journalists or fans. A rebarbative character, not to mention often a slightly menacing s.o.b., Williams, if you had asked him, would have said that it was enough that he was the last man to hit 400; he did it on the field, and therefore didn't have to sell himself off the field. As for his duty to his fans, he didn't see that he had any.'

Do sports stars owe a duty of care to their supporters?

# Stats

## AVERAGE SEASON TICKET PRICES AS A PERCENTAGE OF MEDIAN EARNINGS FOR EACH LEAGUE TWO CLUB'S LOCALITY

| Team | Highest Price (£) | Lowest Price (£) | Average Price (£) | Median Annual Wage (£) | Season Ticket Price as % of Median Earnings (£) |
|---|---|---|---|---|---|
| Accrington Stanley | 276 | 276 | 276.0 | 15,930 | 1.7% |
| Barnet | 380 | 285 | 332.5 | 24,908 | 1.3% |
| Bradford | 138 | 138 | 138.0 | 17,838 | 0.8% |
| Brentford | 400 | 300 | 350.0 | 25,283 | 1.4% |
| Bury | 240 | 200 | 220.0 | 20,712 | 1.1% |
| Chester | 304 | 266 | 285.0 | 21,861 | 1.3% |
| Chesterfield | 410 | 315 | 362.5 | 18,589 | 2.0% |
| Dagenham & Redbridge | 295 | 245 | 270.0 | 23,944 | 1.1% |
| Darlington | 304 | 304 | 304.0 | 18,605 | 1.6% |
| Grimsby | 342 | 304 | 323.0 | 16,462 | 2.0% |
| Hereford | 300 | 260 | 280.0 | 15,490 | 1.8% |
| Lincoln | 335 | 290 | 312.5 | 18,262 | 1.7% |
| Macclesfield | 284 | 220 | 252.0 | 23,532 | 1.1% |
| Mansfield | 320 | 300 | 310.0 | 17,822 | 1.7% |
| MK Dons | 630 | 255 | 442.5 | 22,175 | 2.0% |
| Morecambe | 266 | 228 | 247.0 | 21,237 | 1.2% |
| Notts County | 329 | 255 | 292.0 | 18,179 | 1.6% |
| Peterborough | 425 | 230 | 327.5 | 19,254 | 1.7% |
| Rochdale | 295 | 210 | 252.5 | 19,780 | 1.3% |

| Team | Highest Price (£) | Lowest Price (£) | Average Price (£) | Median Annual Wage (£) | Season Ticket Price as % of Median Earnings (£) |
|------|-------------------|------------------|-------------------|------------------------|--------------------------------------------------|
| Rotherham | 375 | 340 | 357.5 | 18,169 | 2.0% |
| Shrewsbury | 437 | 368 | 402.5 | 18,713 | 2.2% |
| Stockport | 290 | 256 | 273.0 | 20,654 | 1.3% |
| Wrexham | 300 | 275 | 287.5 | 18,236 | 1.6% |
| Wycombe | 335 | 250 | 292.5 | 22,126 | 1.3% |

# Z

**ZEUS, HEAD OF:** 'Nobody taught Bobby. Geniuses, like Beethoven, Shakespeare and Fischer come out of the head of Zeus . . . they seem to be genetically programmed, know before instructed.' John Collins, a tutor at Manhattan Chess club, on Bobby Fischer.

**ZIDANE, ZINEDINE:** Money made from commercial exploitation of his head-butt: €5.6 million.

> Club Apps: 502 **Goals:** 95
> France Apps: 108 **Goals:** 31

£2.30 or £2.50: Cheese is an ever present on the bar menu in the club-house at Troon. 'Two slices of melted cheese with mild cheddar £2.30; two slices of melted cheese with mature cheddar £2.50.' It is all cheese.

**ZIMBABWE:** A troubled nation as Stuart Hall so eloquently explained: 'Don your flannels, black up, play leather on willow with Mugabe cast as a witch doctor. Imagine him out at Lord's casting a curse; tincture of bat's tongues, gorilla's gonads, tiger's testicles . . .' At which point Christian O'Connell interrupted to ask, 'Are we still on air?'

**ZOO:** 'I tried to break his addiction by playing board games with him. He became hooked on Scrabble, spending ages trying to save up the letters for the word "zoo" – he thought it was high-scoring.' Troubled model Amii Grove on Liverpool's Jermaine Pennant.

**ZOO OR NUTS:** Charlton's Greg Halford says, 'If the lads have got *Zoo* or *Nuts* I'll have a read.' His most prized possession is his girlfriend.

# Homework

Mark the following examples of homework and see if you can do better . . .

Man City players have nicknamed Sven 'Alan Partridge' because of his reluctance to move out of his hotel . . . so can we have some suggestions for other sports stars as comedy characters.

- Wayne Rooney as Shrek.

- Colin Montgomery is Eric Cartman – both fat, annoying and mardy.

- Franz Beckenbauer as Jim Royle – both do nothing more than sit on their pimpled arses all day long, moaning and criticising.

### DEFEND THE INDEFENSIBLE
I can't even think about the rugby World Cup this weekend when Kenny Logan is fighting for his life on *Strictly Come Dancing* (to Jeff Probyn, ex-England rugby international).

*or*

The Ryder Cup should be played in Basra.

# Acknowledgements

*Fighting Talk* was born out of a collective frustration with existing sports punditry. Every Saturday morning of the football season we gather together in a tiny studio at BBC TV Centre to put the sporting world to rights. We are very grateful for the support of all our listeners and the following people who have been instrumental in making the show a success: Johnny, Christian, Colin, Dickie, Terry, Gabby, Simon, Giles, Jim, Bob, Moz, Jonathan, Adrian, Michael, Ben, Henry, Dominic, Kamla, Jo, Margaret, Catherine, Hayley, Louise, Charlie, Mike. All the panellists and all the studio managers at BBC Radio 5 live.

Gregor Cameron, Executive Producer